St&

Rers

Business Management
Strategy and Operations

TEN GOLDEN RULES

Other Books by Len Hardy

MARKETING FOR PROFIT

SUCCESSFUL BUSINESS STRATEGY
How to Win in the Market Place

SUCCESSFUL BUSINESS OPERATIONS
How to Develop and Exploit Competitive Advantage

BUSINESS MANAGEMENT
STRATEGY AND OPERATIONS

TEN GOLDEN RULES

LEN HARDY

WINDRUSH BOOKS

First published 1995

Windrush Books Limited
PO Box 5
Kingsbridge
Devon
TQ7 3YB
UK

British Library Cataloguing in Publication Data

A CIP catalogue record for this book is available from the British Library

Library of Congress Cataloging-in-Publication Data

Data has been applied for
ISBN 0-9525626-0-X

Typeset by Paul Stringer, Strood
Printed and bound in Great Britain by
T. J. Press Ltd, Padstow, Cornwall

This book is printed on acid-free paper

To Iris
As always
my love and
my inspiration

Contents

Preface

In my early experience in business, working in medium-sized concerns, I was fortunate in that I was often able to contribute to strategy formulation and also to help 'make it work' in the market-place. I was already in contact with the golden rules although I did not realize it at the time.

In 1957 I was awarded a Leverhulme Research Fellowship. This enabled me to discuss business strategy and operations with many successful business men. The golden rules featured frequently in the discussions. I still remember the sessions and value the time these successful operators were kind enough to give me.

As I moved into more senior positions in business I was able to observe the golden rules in action, and this applied particularly during my period with Lever Bros in the highly competitive soaps and detergents industry.

I was a member of the Lever board for over 20 years, with four years as sales director, six years as marketing director and over ten years as chairman. Business in Lever was always serious, challenging and very enjoyable. It was an ideal place to observe and experience the working of the golden rules. I greatly appreciated the skilled and positive approach of my colleagues in Lever, and also their most willing help.

The views and opinions expressed in this book are, of course, mine and they do not necessarily represent the the views of the Lever company or of the people in it.

This book sets out to help practising business executives, and also students of business, particularly those who have yet to experience the great satisfaction of 'making it work' in the market-place.

Len Hardy

Introduction

If you want to win in business you need a successful strategy backed by effective and efficient operations.

Other factors, such as an inspired leadership, will certainly be of very great value, but skilful strategy formulation and operational efficiency are vitally important. The big question facing a business management intent on success is "How can we be sure to achieve the required level of skill and effectiveness in our strategic planning and operational performance?"

One approach would be to study the writings coming from the professors of the various business schools. Their theories should be worthy of attention, although they may, on occasion, appear to be somewhat abstract and unduly theoretical. Nevertheless, they could be stimulating.

Another approach would be to talk with a number of the business consultants who specialize in providing strategic and operational counsel. Although each consultant tends to have his own particular style and procedure, their views should be helpful.

There are many other approaches that could be beneficial, but possibly the most intriguing, and potentially the most rewarding, would be to talk with a number of experienced and successful operators. Their views could be invaluable, after all they have actually done it, they have been successful in business. They have formed winning strategies and have gone on to make them work in the market-place, the real world of business.

The thoughts of these successful operators are likely to be very 'down to earth' and practical. They are much more likely to be concerned with 'what works' rather than with a highly developed set of theories. Normally these people will be more inclined to talk of their views rather than to express them in lengthy writings.

■ *My personal experience tells me that the successful operators would talk in terms of the golden rules as described in this book. They know that if you want to survive and to prosper in business you have to win – and in the final analysis the golden rules are really all about winning.*

The Golden Rules

All trades, professions, and practices build up what are often referred to as 'lores'. The *Oxford English Dictionary* talks of a 'lore' as 'a body of tradition and knowledge on a subject'. In this book we are concerned with a series of 'lores' for business strategy and operations. They have been called 'golden rules' here as this tends to be a more readily understood and accepted description.

■ *The golden rules are based on the record, and are established over time and from experience. They live, and go on living, because basically they are right. If something should develop which means that they are no longer basically right, then they will fade and die. Only if they are right are they worthy of remembering and quoting.*

Frequently the golden rules for a particular practice owe much to those that have been developed for a similar activity which has a longer history of systematic study. Where the considerations have much in common, this is understandable.

Many of the golden rules for business strategy have their origins in the long established 'rules' for military strategy and operations.

The military are concerned with war, and in many ways business is a form of war. If you are to be successful in a war you will need to out-think and out-manoeuvre your enemy. You may need to move faster than he does so that your forces are in an advantageous position from which to dictate the course and outcome of the action. Very similar requirements can apply if you want to be successful in business where the enemy are your competitors.

The golden rules are invariably contained within simple statements. They have to be simple if they are to be remembered and repeated. Sometimes the issues with which the 'rules' are concerned appear to be very complex and so the charge of over-simplification is often levelled against them. There is some truth in the charge, but at the same time it misunderstands the real purpose and value of the 'rules'.

Even the most complex of business proposals can usually be analysed down to a small number of 'key' considerations, and it is with these considerations that the golden rules are primarily concerned.

There is also an argument that the golden rules are merely common sense. If they are then this is surely a great compliment to them. In business, as in so many other walks of life, common sense is often a commodity that is in short supply. If the golden rules spell out, and impress upon those who become acquainted with them, good business common sense, then they have fulfilled a particularly valuable service.

Using the Golden Rules

The golden rules do not tell you how to form a successful strategy or how to become a truly effective operator. Successful business strategy formulation, and effective operation, is both a science and an art.

Highly successful strategies have been formulated on the back of an envelope; they have also been formulated after extensive and detailed research. There is no one correct way to formulate a successful strategy. However, in the process of forming a strategic plan, whether by use of an envelope back or a detailed planning process, there will be a need to assess the opportunities available, and to consider the ability of the company and of its competitors to develop competitive advantages that will provide the basis for the exploitation of the opportunities. Then follows the task of selecting for action those opportunities that the business expects to be able to develop and exploit more effectively than its competitors.

■ *The selection task is vitally important. Get it right and business success can follow. Get it wrong and worthwhile success will be impossible.*

It is during the selection process that the golden rules can make a very major contribution. Any proposal that goes against the reasoning of a golden rule should be suspect and be subjected to a particularly rigorous review.

In effect, the golden rules can act as a form of sieve through which the various proposals for investment and action should be passed. Those that get through will have passed their opening test. It does not follow that they should automatically be adopted for action if they pass – other outstanding reasons for rejection may appear – but at least they will have taken the first step towards action.

The Golden Rules Apply to All Businesses, in All Markets

The golden rules discussed in this book are clearly not the only rules of business strategy and operations. Some business managers may argue they are not necessarily the most important rules; but I am sure it would be generally agreed that they are certainly among the most important.

In this book many of the examples and illustrations used have been taken from the consumer goods industry. This is primarily because a large part of my own practical experience has been in the consumer goods markets and so I find it easier to relate the golden rules to this type and form of operation.

■ *However, one of the great strengths of the golden rules is that they apply across all markets. They are applicable to all types and forms of business.*

One of the golden rules states that "the pursuit (i.e. the follow-up) is as important as the initial attack". For the producer of, for instance, a new brand of chocolate bar or toilet soap, this will quickly be appreciated. The importance of the pursuit for the machine tool manufacturer, or the insurance company that introduces a new series of policies will, after consideration, be equally clear. It may take a different form, but its basic purpose will be the same.

Similar remarks apply for all the golden rules. They can help the soaps and detergent manufacturer, the builder, the retailer, indeed they are of significance for all business people.

All of the golden rules are applicable to strategic and operational considerations. This is understandable if it is accepted that the same basic principles will be involved in considering proposals under either heading. The time period for strategy proposals is likely to be a longer one than for operations, and also the investment involved can be expected to be at a higher level. Of course, operations are within the business strategy, and their objectives will be concerned with the requirements of the strategy.

The Golden Rules are Backed by Sound Business Economics

For many readers this book will be their first introduction to the golden rules as such. However, they may well have heard one or more of the rules quoted as part of the discussion which has considered a particular business proposal.

It is quite probable that the quote will have come from one of the older and more senior members of the review group, and there will have been a temptation for the younger members to dismiss the quote as 'the old man riding one of his favourite hobby horses again'. The younger members need to be careful with their comments.

■ *The golden rules are invariably backed by sound business economics. The rules have come into being because they have been proved 'right' over time, and this means they have been 'right' in terms of business economics.*

The position brings to mind the old countryman who reminds his visitor that "A red sky at night means a shepherd's delight, there will be a fine day tomorrow". The countryman makes the comment because he has observed over many years that a red sky is invariably followed by a fine day. In fact, the meteorologist is able to show that there is very good scientific reason why a fine day should follow a red sky.

As the golden rules are examined more closely in the chapters which follow, their sound economic basis will become very evident.

Should You Ever Move Against a Golden Rule?

Is it possible to move against a golden rule and to go on and achieve a real business success? The answer to this question must be a clear "Yes". However, the golden rules are basically right and so if you move against their reasoning you are unlikely to record a real success. You may manage a degree of success, but it is most unlikely to be at a fully satisfactory level.

■ *If you decide to go against a golden rule then you need to have one or more factors within your business proposal, and they will need to be 'key' factors, that are markedly superior to those of your competitors. The strength of these factor/s will need to be such that they have the ability to carry the proposition to success despite shortcomings in other aspects.*

The outstanding example of such a superior 'key' factor would be where a new brand is launched against the dominant leader of an established market. Such a move would be clearly against the golden rule NEVER ATTACK A DOMINANT LEADER HEAD-ON. However, if the new brand had a significant competitive advantage in product performance which was protected by law (e.g. a patent), then the move against the leader could possibly succeed. And the success could be recorded without a fully competent launch, or pricing policy, or fully effective production facilities. The competitive advantage held by the new brand would need to be of very real significance, and its protection would need to be fully secure.

The manufacturer in this example would have been justified in moving against the golden rule. In circumstances of this kind there are two vitally important questions that need to be asked and answered – first, "Just how significant is my competitive advantage?"

and second, "Can I give my advantage satisfactory protection?". It is clearly of great importance to the manufacturer that he should get his answers to these questions 'right' before deciding to take action. Only if the competitive advantage is strong enough to carry the proposition against the entrenched leader, and can be given satisfactory protection, should the move be made.

Of course, you can never be absolutely sure of the strength of your competitive advantage. Research, testing and other such activities can be helpful in providing guidance, but in the final analysis a judgement decision will be necessary.

It is also difficult to be completely sure that you can provide satisfactory protection. Even the most steadfast of defences can sometimes be breached, and so again sound judgement will be required.

Clearly, sound judgement, and possibly also some good fortune, will be essential if you are ever to achieve real success 'against the rules'. The problems, and the opportunities, of a move 'against the rules' are discussed in more detail in the chapters which follow.

The Golden Rules: Principles and Techniques

There is a view which argues that the golden rules were fine in the 1960s and 70s, and possibly in the 1980s, but for the 90s and beyond they are unlikely to apply. The prime reasons often quoted in support of the view are the rapid changes in technology now experienced, and the highly developed reasoning and approach of the many progressive managers now operating in business.

In considering this view it is important to differentiate between principles and techniques. Principles are considerations of basic significance. They go to the root of the matter; they serve as a foundation from which other views and approaches are developed. Invariably principles are formed and tested through time. Once established they continue to apply into the longer term.

A technique is a mode of execution. It is a way of achieving a particular objective. Techniques can be very effective in business when they are used wisely, but they can come and go rapidly. Unlike principles they are often influenced by the fashion of the day.

■ *The golden rules are principles. They most certainly apply in the 1990s and will do so well beyond.*

Brands

Within the chapters in which the golden rules are discussed the terms 'brands' and 'products' are mentioned frequently. The terms are given a wider meaning, and a greater significance, than is usually accredited to them. An explanation is necessary.

Some brands are well-known household names and are sold to consumers via the retail trade, with the support of extensive advertising and promotion. Other brands are of a different nature – they may be, for instance, machine tools, life assurance policies, or a plumbing service – but they are all brands, and they have a number of significant factors in common.

A brand is a name. If the manufacturer has done a good branding job the name will come to represent in the consumer's mind the fulfilment of a purpose, a standard of performance in meeting the purpose, a price-level, and a personality. Over time, brands, like people, develop personalities. It is important that the personality should be the *right* one for once it is formed it is very difficult to change.

■ *Brands exploit marketing opportunities. Brands provide the company's revenue and without revenue profit is impossible. Through its brands the company makes the direct contact with its ultimate customer, the consumer. The company is judged by its brands. They are all vitally important to a company and should be developed with great care and attention – strong brands should mean a strong company.*

The Order of Discussion

This book discusses each one of the ten golden rules in turn. For each one the discussion is relatively short – it could be argued that every one of the rules deserves a book for itself. The aim here has been to cover the 'key' considerations for each rule.

The rules are not discussed in an order of importance. In practice, their importance will be linked to the occasion and circumstances in which they apply.

The intention has been to consider the background for each particular rule, the business economics that support it, and the specific circumstances in which it is most likely to apply.

The book sets out to remind practising business executives of the golden rules. Many of them will be known to these executives. The 'old man' in their particular company may have been keen on their application and quoted them frequently. However, whether their executives have a knowledge of the rules or not, the record shows that many businesses, even those that are considered to be well managed, are guilty of breaking the rules.

Frequent attempts have been made to attack the brand leader head-on, and frequently they have failed. And on many occasions in their haste to be 'first', some of the most experienced managers have forgotten the importance of also being 'right'.

The difficult economic conditions of recent periods have also acted to tempt certain operators to engage in price wars without the appropriate preparation. Again the activities have frequently proven to be both painful and costly. The golden rule warns against entering a price war 'unless you can be sure you will win'.

If this book encourages practising business executives to recall the golden rules when they are considering a business proposal, and to remember that if they propose to move against one of the golden rules they need to be sure they have much more than just a good case, then it will have served a most valuable purpose.

For many of those who are students of business this book is likely to be their first introduction to the golden rules. In their studies they may well have covered certain of the fundamental economic considerations which go to form the base of a particular rule, but they are unlikely to have studied the rules as such.

An early introduction to the golden rules must surely be beneficial to the students. Better to come to terms with them through study rather than after a number of expensive failures in the hard school of practical experience.

Chapter 1

Stick to the 'Knitting'

*but firstly be sure you
know just what is your 'knitting'*

The golden rule STICK TO THE 'KNITTING' has been quoted over many years, but it clearly owes much of its recent prominence to the fact that it is featured in Peters and Waterman's best-selling business management book *In Search of Excellence*.

The book is an examination of the behaviour and practices of a group of businesses the authors had identified as among 'America's best-run companies'. The authors are very forthright on the results of their studies for this particular subject. They say: "Our principal finding is clear and simple. Organizations that do branch out (whether by acquisition or internal diversification) but stick very close to their knitting outperform the others." They go on to quote other well-respected research studies which agree with their conclusions.

The record backs this view very strongly. It has been noticeable that during the recession years of 1990–93 the financial columns of the U.K. newspapers have talked repeatedly of companies, many of them regarded as well-managed, returning to their 'core' activities ('core' is used here as synonymous with 'knitting'). The return has often been a difficult and very expensive experience. If these companies had 'stuck to their knitting' much of the difficulty, and the expense, could have been avoided.

■ *The basic reasoning that supports this golden rule is the simple fact that a particular management can become highly skilled in the specific sphere of business operations which is its 'knitting'. Over time the managers come to appreciate which are the 'key' considerations; their judgements in the area become finely tuned and very reliable. They know when to be particularly aggressive and when to be defensive in their marketing activities. Their experience in the area is such that they have already witnessed the 'big mistakes' once, and are not likely to allow them to be repeated. Surprises are possible, but they are likely to be small ones.*

New markets, new activities and new processes can all bring abstruse and very painful surprises. In the new areas, the important judgement decisions are more difficult. The experience, gained over long periods and so valuable in the traditional markets, is missing in the new fields. Competitors may be of a different kind, distribution channels more varied, and customers more fickle.

The new operations invariably require more top management time than was planned, unforeseen production problems arise, financial estimates go wrong, and so on. All of this means that success is that much more difficult to achieve.

Beyond this there is the great danger that the earlier excitement and novelty of the new project, and the later problems it brings, will detract from the effort and skill placed behind the established business and soon they will be in trouble.

The message is clear: if business management wants success it should STICK TO THE 'KNITTING'. It should spurn the temptations, even those which appear attractive, to venture into new fields. It should stick to those areas where it is skilled and experienced.

This all sounds very simple and straightforward. Clearly the golden rule STICK TO THE 'KNITTING' should be obeyed. But is it quite so simple? No it is not, and further discussion is necessary.

Just What is the 'Knitting'?

■ *The instruction* STICK TO THE 'KNITTING' *is simple enough if the management concerned are aware of just what is their 'knitting'.*

The fact is that in the majority of companies the management has never taken the trouble to answer the question "What is our knitting?" It is highly likely that in a typical company among the senior staff there will be a whole series of different views as to what constitutes the 'knitting' of their particular business. It is very difficult to STICK TO THE 'KNITTING' when you are not clear just what your knitting is.

This specific golden rule has come to be widely respected, and one which many managements would now claim to follow. Clearly if they are really serious about this they need to come to recognize just what is their 'knitting'.

As we examine this requirement in more detail we shall come to appreciate that the recognition task is certainly not an elementary one. There is no one correct definition for every company operating in a particular market, or for companies of a specific size, or for those practising a certain management approach.

It is suggested that the 'knitting' of each individual company will be specific to that company. It may be very close to that of other similar businesses, but there will be differences. These differences, although very small, will often be of significance.

The proposal which is developed here is that the 'knitting' is clearly connected with the people of the business, often a very small number of people, possibly just one person. It is about the skills and abilities possessed by these people and their use in the management of the business.

Defining the 'knitting' of a company as well-known as Procter and Gamble would appear to be simple. The company is involved in the large-scale manufacture and marketing of fast moving consumer brands. Surely, this is its 'knitting'.

The company is widely recognized as a very well-managed business. It has been awarded many accolades for good management by business journals, management associations, and other similar bodies. It is well respected on Wall Street.

Procter and Gamble is one of the companies featured in *In Search of Excellence*. In one passage of the book, Ed Harness, a former head of P&G, is quoted as saying "This company has never left its base. We seek to be anything but a conglomerate." In effect, P&G believes in sticking to its 'knitting'.

The company is in many ways very secretive about its more detailed approach to business management and in particular to its business operations. Very few companies have issued a statement which attempts to set out in detail just what they believe their 'knitting' to be; P&G is certainly not an exception to this general position. However, it is interesting to speculate on what such a statement from P&G would contain. It is possible that it might surprise many observers.

'Knitting' in Procter and Gamble

Procter and Gamble's skill in marketing is recognized throughout the world. Its disciplined and effective approach to advertising is strongly praised. In selling its brands it is known to have a well-developed and straightforward approach which has brought impressive results. The company is understandably proud of its 'close contact with the consumer'. In the field of marketing research its reputation is high.

Beyond this it is known to have considerable skills in production engineering and in the large-scale manufacture and distribution of relatively simple consumer products.

From all of this it would seem reasonable to say that P&G's knitting is concerned with the large-scale manufacture and marketing of fast moving, relatively simple consumer brands. However, it is suggested that it is necessary to go beyond this statement if the company's real 'knitting' is to be discovered.

Over recent periods P&G has had many successes and few failures. The outstanding successes have invariably been occasions when the company has been able to use its undoubted skills in large-scale production and marketing on a product into which its research and development laboratory has been able to build a significant competitive advantage. This advantage has usually taken the form of a particular performance attribute which is well appreciated by the consumer.

This consideration is evidenced by the conspicuous success with

Tide in the U.S.A. The brand had outstanding performance attributes and was able to make great strides forward in the development of the synthetic detergent market. Similarly the toothpaste *Crest* became the leading brand in the U.S. market after certain of its technological qualities has been recognized by the American Dental Association and marketed strongly by P&G. In Europe the detergent brand *Ariel* was able to exploit the performance advantages provided by its biological formula and to become a highly successful brand.

In all of these successes, the P&G manufacturing and marketing skills were exploiting the work of the research and development laboratory. In each case the laboratory had provided a product 'extra' which facilitated the development of a significant competitive advantage.

A P&G venture that many observers would consider as unsuccessful, was the purchase of Crush International in 1980. This marked the entry of the company as a serious competitor into the U.S. soft drinks market.

This particular venture would appear, at first sight, to be 'knitting' for P&G. It was a large and growing consumer market, very much a market where highly skilled marketing could make a major contribution. In particular, it was a market where effective consumer advertising would have a substantial part to play. P&G was, of course, very strong in each of these specific skills.

And yet the company announced in 1989 that the Crush International business was for sale; it was in fact sold in 1990. The business had made no real progress in terms of market share, and it was certainly not thought to have been a success in trading profit terms.

When P&G moved into the soft drinks market they were expected to be successful. The company has not disclosed in any detail why it decided to withdraw.

Outside observers have speculated on the P&G operations in the soft drinks market. They agree the competition was strong – Coca-Cola and Pepsi-Cola are known to be exceptionally difficult adversaries – but P&G has been able to cope with difficult competitors in other markets.

It would seem to be agreed that the company met two particularly troublesome areas within its operations.

Although the P&G research and development laboratory was able to introduce a number of product innovations into the company brands, they were not able to develop an innovation that could rank as a 'significant competitive advantage' in terms of consumer acceptance of Crush soft drinks. As a result the brand advertising and other presentation never worked in the manner, or at the level of effectiveness, that the company would normally expect, certainly not at the level of effectiveness it achieved in its other successful operations.

Secondly, P&G experienced considerable difficulties with the manufacturing and distribution system which applied for Crush and within the soft drinks market generally.

Operators in the U.S. soft drinks market tend to distribute their brands through bottlers. Each bottler has the exclusive right for bottling (i.e. manufacturing) and distributing the brand over an agreed area. The bottlers are clearly 'key' people who need to be handled with care, and given the right form and degree of motivation. In its established markets P&G would normally carry out the full manufacture of its brands, and then sell them through its own sales force and have overall control of their physical distribution to the appropriate warehouses and stores. The company never appeared to be happy with the 'via bottler' system. It ran experiments which seemed to be aimed at by-passing the local bottler. There were disagreements and at least one bottler was thought to be considering legal action.

Two vitally important parts of the Crush operation were *not* 'knitting' for P&G. And it would seem reasonable to conclude that in the Crush venture the company was not STICKING TO THE KNITTING.

■ *It can be reasoned that P&G's 'knitting' is concerned with more than just the large-scale manufacture and marketing of consumer brands. The company's 'knitting' also involves an ability to bring a suitably effective research and development contribution to the operation so that significant competitive advantages can be produced and in this way the company's highly skilled marketing ability is allowed to do a full exploitation in the market-place.*

P&G is also skilled in a particular form of production, selling and distribution which is part of its 'knitting'.

The salient point is that this 'knitting' is specific to P&G. It is directly related to the skills and abilities of the people managing and operating within the P&G business.

'Knitting' in Cadbury-Schweppes

The Cadbury-Schweppes company is an interesting example of a business which apparently redefined its 'knitting' and then took action accordingly. The company was an amalgamation in 1969 of Cadbury, a leading U.K. manufacturer and marketer of chocolate and other forms of confectionery, and Schweppes, one of the foremost businesses in the soft drinks industry.

The company moved into other areas and in the early 1980s had additional businesses covering food, tea, health and hygiene. All the various businesses in the company were concerned with the large-scale manufacture and marketing of relatively low priced, fast moving consumer brands. Although each business may have had certain special avenues of distribution, all were using grocery stores as a major avenue. All of the businesses used advertising extensively to attract consumers to their brands.

If the Cadbury-Schweppes 'knitting' was defined broadly as 'manufacturing and marketing fast moving consumer brands' then it could be agreed that the company was 'sticking to the knitting' when it moved into the new consumer businesses. However, the new businesses enjoyed only limited success and in 1986 they were sold. From then on Cadbury-Schweppes decided to concentrate on its two basic operating areas of confectionery and soft drinks.

In the following years the company made a number of new acquisitions. They were all in the chocolate/confectionery field or in soft drinks.

■ *Clearly Cadbury-Schweppes had decided its 'knitting' was more than just the large-scale manufacture and marketing of consumer brands. This was part of the 'knitting', but only part. Beyond this there was a need to develop superior products, products that could offer the consumer something 'extra'. The 'extra' could become a significant competitive advantage, and go on to bring about a superior level of profitability.*

The position would appear to be somewhat similar to that for Procter and Gamble. The 'extra' concerned would normally require investment, and a skilled application, in research and development.

It is probable that Cadbury-Schweppes possessed these necessary skills in its original chocolate/confectionery business and in soft drinks, but did not have them at a satisfactory level in the other businesses.

Without the 'extra' higher level profits would have been difficult to obtain. And so Cadbury-Schweppes redefined its 'knitting' and concentrated its efforts on confectionery and soft drinks. With its new acquisitions it was careful to STICK TO THE 'KNITTING'.

'Knitting' in Hanson Trust

Defining the 'knitting' for manufacturing and marketing companies such as Procter and Gamble and Cadbury-Schweppes is relatively easy when compared with the task of deciding what is the 'knitting' of a complex business such as that of a well-established conglomerate.

One of the most successful conglomerates of recent years is Hanson Trust. Originally formed as a private company in 1950, it was converted into a public company and its shares issued on the London Stock Exchange in 1964.

Over a period of some 40 years Hanson has made remarkable progress. It is now a major business in both the U.S.A. and the U.K. Its operating companies cover brickmaking, engineering, footwear, furniture and furnishings, housewares, garden equipment, and many other fields. In the year to 30 September 1989 Hanson's reported profit (before tax) had moved to over £1bn, and in 1994 it exceeded £1.3bn.

What is Hanson's 'knitting'? It is certainly not limited to a particular industry or market – Hanson operates successfully in many. It is not in a special form of manufacture or distribution – Hanson operates successfully across a broad spectrum.

Much has been written of Hanson's concentration within its operating companies on markets and products that are relatively simple. Rarely, if ever, does it allow its companies to become involved in 'hi-tech' projects that require extensive research and development and where long 'pay-out' periods are common. Hanson wants its operating companies to be strong cash contributors and, as far as is possible, free of high risk.

Hanson has also gained a reputation as a conglomerate that allows its operating companies considerable freedom in day-to-day management, but also enforces very strict financial controls. Hanson company managers are expected to meet their profit and cash targets.

While these two considerations (i.e. the choice of industry and market where the company is to operate, and the strict enforcement of financial controls) may well be important factors in Hanson's success it would be wrong to consider them as 'knitting'.

The financial controls are really concerned with the effective management of the operating companies. They are clearly seen by Hanson as a factor of consequence in the success of the companies, but they are certainly not the only factor or necessarily the most important.

It is suggested that if the successful Hanson operation is considered in detail over the longer term it will be seen that its success is linked closely to five operations:

1. An ability to identify undervalued and/or underemployed assets.
2. The skill to purchase the identified assets at an advantageous price.
3. A clarity of purpose in deciding which assets should be retained and operated, and which should be sold on.
4. An ability to get an advantageous price for the assets to be sold.
5. The skill to select, appoint, and to motivate, managers who have the ability to operate the assets which are retained effectively.

In all its successful operations Hanson has carried out these five tasks effectively and in a coordinated manner. This is what Hanson is good at. This is surely Hanson's 'knitting'.

The effective completion of items 1 and 2 is clearly fundamental to any total success that Hanson is to achieve. If it should make a mistake and buy assets that are over-valued then it will have difficulty in working them and making a satisfactory return. If it overpays for the assets it is unlikely to be able to sell them on profitably. If the assets are already fully employed then there is no leeway to make gains from additional utilization.

Hanson never appears to be in doubt as to which business it should sell and which it should retain. The cynic will say that if the price is right any business is for sale, and this is probably correct; however, Hanson is clearly pleased to sell some companies quickly, while with others there is no hurry.

In general, Hanson would seem to be interested in retaining businesses which have relatively simple products, a low level of research and development, and an ability to generate a strong cash flow. Such businesses tend to be low risk and to fit well with the Hanson approach to strict financial control. Hanson has demonstrated an ability to manage this type of business most effectively.

In practice, Hanson has been prepared to leave its operating subsidiaries to get on with the job of delivering results. The managers of the businesses are expected to meet the various agreed financial targets. If they do this they are well rewarded and left alone – if they fail then head office can be expected to take firm action.

The fact that Hanson has been able to make this form of operation work successfully would seem to verify that it has exercised considerable skill in the selection and motivation of its operating managers. The ability to get an advantageous price for the assets to be sold centres on a number of factors including a well-developed knowledge of the particular market concerned, a willingness to be sensibly patient, and a fully competent skill in negotiation. Hanson has clearly possessed these various attributes.

The important point is that Hanson is only operating at its full potential when it concentrates its activities on following through each of the five considerations. It is possible that a satisfactory result could accrue to Hanson if just one or two of the five are completed skilfully. But a totally effective operation requires that all five be completed successfully.

■ *When Hanson restricts its operations to the five listed consider-*
ations, it is 'sticking to the knitting'. If it allows its attentions and
activities to stray into other areas it will be moving away from its
'knitting' and, if the golden rule is accepted, will be much more likely
to find trouble.

It is important to appreciate the difference between the 'knitting'
for the successful conglomerate and that of the successful operating
company. 'Knitting' for the operating company is invariably directly
linked to particular operating skills in specific markets: skills in research and development, in marketing, and in other definite areas
can be of major significance.

For the conglomerate, as we have seen with Hanson, the 'knitting'
is more likely to be concerned with factors such as financial adroit-
ness, skilful evaluation, stock market 'feel', and shrewd, very able
negotiation.

When conglomerates attempt to become operating companies they
invariably fail – this is why part of the Hanson 'knitting' is concerned
with the careful selection of those assets which are to be retained, and
then the skilful selection of the managers who are to operate those
assets. Management by 'financial control' (the approach usually followed by successful conglomerates) tends to be much easier with
'simple' products than it is with those of a 'hi-tech' nature.

Equally, operating companies frequently fail when they attempt to
become, in part, conglomerates. They rarely have the appropriate
skills required to manage their new acquisitions successfully. They
often attempt to apply the measures and the approach that has
worked well in their established markets. However, conditions, customers, competitors, and other factors are rarely the same in the new
field and the approach fails. They should STICK TO THE KNITTING.

The 'Knitting' – A Definition

Clearly it is vitally important that a company should be able to define
correctly just what is its 'knitting'.

■ *Management of the company will normally be tempted to believe its 'knitting' is much wider in coverage than it really is. "A good manager is a good manager anywhere" is a somewhat flattering statement that many managers would like to believe, but it can be very misleading. It ignores the fact than many of the 'key' decisions in business are judgement decisions. The record shows that a well-developed skill, backed by a sound experience in the particular area concerned, can be a considerable aid to getting the all important judgements right. The number of managers who have been really successful in a variety of markets and industries is very limited.*

One of the outstanding instances of incorrect 'knitting' definition is the oft quoted case of the U.S. railroads. Certain of the major railroads, who had a successful record, were convinced that their 'knitting' was the provision of transportation. Working to this belief they became heavily involved in the U.S. civil airline business in its early development period. The moves were in the main unsuccessful. The railroad companies had made an error in defining their 'knitting'. They were not in the transportation business, they were in the railroad business. It was in running railroads that they had exceptional skills; operating railroads was their 'knitting'.

Even the definition of 'operating railroads' was not fully satisfactory. It was clear that some of the railroads had considerable skills in operating rail systems that specialized in short-run passenger services; others had skills in managing systems that specialized in long-distance heavy goods traffic, and there were other specializations. In the case of each railroad there was a need to define the 'knitting' beyond the simple 'operating a railroad'.

It is clear that a company's 'knitting' is something that it can do particularly well. Beyond this it is something that the company has shown it can do more than once – that is, it is something the company has the ability to repeat.

With this in mind, and also the other issues that have been considered, we can now attempt a definition of a company's 'knitting':

■ *A company's 'knitting' is that specific business operation, or series of operations, that it has demonstrated an ability to perform, and to keep performing, at a level of effectiveness which is superior to that of its competitors.*

This is a short and simple definition and some further explanation is necessary. The term business operation should be interpreted in a wide form. For instance, it could include research and development investment, financial operations, marketing research, and similar activities which may not always be considered as business operations.

It is important that the company has proven its ability to perform the 'knitting' successfully, and then to repeat it with the same success. Beyond this there is a need to demonstrate an ability to perform at a superior level.

The term competitor as used in the definition should include any other business that is capable of competing in the particular field, and not merely those businesses that are already competing.

Stick to the 'Knitting' Applies in Banking

In the U.K., through the immediate post-war years and on into the 1960s and 1970s, the TSB (Trustee Savings Bank) achieved considerable prominence as a well-managed and successful savings bank. It specialized in having relatively small and medium-size branches in cities and towns throughout the country. Its customers were, in the main, small to medium-level savers. The TSB was floated on the London Stock Exchange in 1986.

To its normal banking business the TSB had been able to add other services such as insurance and mortgage provision, and these fitted well with its basic approach. It had also added a credit card and a hire purchase business. To a considerable extent these additional businesses were utilizing the established customer base of the savings bank.

In 1987 the TSB purchased the merchant banking group Hill Samuel. TSB was a savings bank and so this was a move outside of its 'knitting'.

On 3 February 1992, under the heading 'Anatomy of a banking nightmare' this is how the *Financial Times* commented on the TSB position:

There is no better cautionary tale for bankers than TSB Group's ill-fated foray into commercial lending. It is the story of a savings bank which got into a business, corporate lending, whose risks it did not properly appreciate.

It then lent too much too quickly and concentrated much of the lending on a particularly risky sector, property.

The price of this mistake has been high. The bank recently disclosed an annual loss of £47m, in large part because it made provisions of £432m to cover possible losses on commercial loans made by its subsidiary, Hill Samuel.

These provisions were equivalent to 9 per cent of Hill Samuel's loan portfolio, a very high rate. But just over four years ago, TSB was confident that by paying £777m for Hill Samuel, it would shed its dowdy image as a savings bank and pose a challenge to England's quartet of clearing banks.

It can now claim close kinship with the clearing banks, but not in the way it wanted. As a proportion of its total loan book, its losses from corporate lending are even bigger than theirs. The group would be in trouble without its unglamorous traditional business.

The golden rule clearly does apply to banking. It would not be unreasonable to argue that the TSB should have stuck to the 'knitting'.

The Business Without 'Knitting'

A question which is sure to arise from the definition of 'knitting' is "What is the position of a company that does not have an operation which it performs at a superior level?" There will, of course, be many such companies.

A company that does not have 'knitting' as described here will always find it difficult to earn a satisfactory level of profit. It can be argued that as it does not have the ability to perform a business operation at a superior level then it does not deserve to receive a higher level of profit. It is important to appreciate that a business does not have to be a market leader, or highly profitable, to have 'knitting'.

The small company supplying a special, but very small, segment of a market with a product that is formulated in a particular manner has its 'knitting' – in its special sector it is probably a superior performer. Frequently the problem for such a company is that it is not concentrating enough of its effort on the 'knitting' – many of its activities will probably be centred on brands and operations which are not 'knitting', and these will consume a disproportionate amount of resources in relation to the return they contribute.

Companies without 'knitting' can often continue to trade over a long period of time because their owners are prepared to accept a low level of return on the investment they have in the business. However, such companies are always very vulnerable to attack from effective competitors. Their low level of return means they have very little margin of safety in their operation.

Can a Move to Invest Outside the 'Knitting' be Justified?

Should it become clear to the business management that further investment in the 'knitting' is unlikely to bring a satisfactory profit return then there are two possible uses for any available funds:

1. An investment in a project that is outside the 'knitting'.
2. A return of funds to shareholders.

The golden rule says very clearly STICK TO THE 'KNITTING' and so it follows that any proposal to commit funds outside the 'knitting' should undergo a particularly rigorous examination.

Before dismissing the 'knitting' as no longer able to provide a satisfactory return management should always be prepared to take a 'second look'. Frequently companies find that with suitable innovation – new design, new mechanical operation, new presentation, and so on – what at first appears to be the end of the 'knitting' can, in fact, be extended, and the extension can be very profitable.

Of course, over the years, there have been many notable moves outside the 'knitting' which have proved successful. The golden rules are usually right, but not always.

The requirement is that any proposal to move outside the 'knitting' should be subjected to a rigorous review, and that if it is to go forward for action it should come through with very confident backing.

The important questions to be asked will include "How strong is our competitive advantage?", "Is it strong enough to do the job we require of it?" and "Can we give it a satisfactory level of protection?" Beyond this there will be questions as to whether or not the necessary reserves are available to cover both the attack on the market and the pursuit, and also the level of profit return which can be expected. If the answers to these questions are favourable then the proposition should at least be worthy of detailed consideration.

The temptation to move away from the 'knitting' is always present. The other markets always appear easy, the competition weak, and the margins good. Of course, it rarely works out to be as simple, as easy, and as profitable as it at first appears.

A move which would seem to have a better chance of success is one where a company is able to move into an entirely new market in which at least a major part of its existing 'knitting' can be utilized. If the market is a new one there will be no established companies that have built up a 'knitting' position within it.

In the U.K. the Mars Company was established as a leading competitor in the chocolate/confectionery market. The company had built up a very high reputation in marketing, particularly in consumer research and advertising. In addition, the company was known to have well-developed skills in selling, and also in high-volume production.

The Mars company moved into the 'new' U.K. petfood market during its early development period. Much of the company's 'knitting' in confectionery was applicable to this new business – this applied particularly in marketing, advertising, selling, and high-volume production. The company was able to develop additional skills in such areas as product research and development, and raw material purchase. As the market was 'new' there was no established business with a 'knitting' position.

The Mars move into petfood in the U.K., a move which was at the time outside its 'knitting', has proved to be highly successful.

An investment project which is 'outside the knitting' is invariably a higher risk project. It follows that if a considerable part of the operation of this new project can be included as 'knitting' then the risk will be reduced.

The great danger when it is recognized that further investment in the 'knitting' is not advisable is that the business management will cast around for an 'attractive' project. The investment will not be 'knitting' and it may be made in a hurry – individually both factors can bring trouble, together they are almost sure to. There is a need to plan ahead so that the business is ready with alternative proposals well before it becomes clear that the 'knitting' is unlikely to be worthy of further investment.

When a company has a new development, or the basis of a development with which it could be successful, in an 'out of knitting' market, it could well decide to obtain a 'learning experience' in the new field before moving ahead with market-place action.

This would mean, for instance, the purchase of a small business already operating in the market. Personnel would be transferred into the business with a view to their gaining a 'learning experience' of the new markets, and also helping to develop the business so that it will be capable of mounting a large-scale attack within a suitable time.

An approach of this kind has much to recommend it. One of the most important considerations is that the time and attention of managers in the base company should not be diverted. It is also a fact that the personnel who have the opportunity to participate in the 'learning experience' are likely to benefit greatly from it in terms of their wider managerial development. What the 'learning experience' approach does, in effect, is to transfer the new project proposal into a unit where it can be legitimately described as 'knitting'.

Of course, it needs to be appreciated that entry into a 'learning experience' of this kind is certainly not a guarantee of success. It can be argued that Procter and Gamble followed a form of this approach with their move into the soft drinks market (quoted above) but it failed. However, it should also be noted that when the same company used the approach to enter the paper market (P&G purchased the medium-sized business of Charmin as a prelude to their wider activities in paper) the move would appear to have served them very well.

Stick to the 'Knitting': Utilities are not Exempt

Under the headline 'Utilities write off £1bn on failed diversification spree', *The Sunday Times*, in the Business Section within its edition for 15 May 1994, reported as follows:

> Britain's privatised water and electricity companies are heading for more heavy write-downs and losses after last week's announcement by East Midlands Electricity that it has written off £80m on its widely criticised diversification programme and is making 700 people redundant.
>
> Analysts now reckon that since privatisation, the 10 water companies and 12 regional electricity companies (RECs) have spent about £1.6 billion on businesses outside their main core areas, of which more than £1 billion has been written off (much of it as goodwill). On a combined turnover of £2.7 billion, the diversified interests made a total loss of £51m last year. It will be even higher this year.
>
> SG Warburg, the investment house, in a report on the last full set of accounts for both sectors, says the performance of both industries outside their core areas is becoming worse rather than better. The water companies in particular are expected to be forced into further write-offs at an embarrassing time as the industry approaches the review by the Ofwat regulator, Ian Byatt.
>
> "The sector will enter the periodic review of price-cap factors losing money from non-core businesses – hardly a positive flag for either regulator or investor," Warburg said. City analysts now estimate the water sector will only generate a positive after-tax contribution from non-core activities in 1995–96 at the earliest.
>
> East Midlands' write-offs and losses on diversification made analysts downgrade their forecasts for 1993–94 profits from £185m to £55m. Six of the 12 electricity companies reported a loss in non-core activities in 1992–93; that figure will probably rise this year.

Clearly, utilities should obey the golden rule and STICK TO THE 'KNITTING'.

People and the 'Knitting'

It is very clear that a company's 'knitting' is closely linked with the people of the business and their skills. All of the people of the business are concerned, but there is a special significance which applies to the management.

The way the 'people factor' features within the 'knitting' is of consequence. There are two broad approaches:

1. Systematic.
2. Personal.

Under a systematic approach, the people factor is created through a form of personnel, and in particular management, development. For instance, within the marketing department a series of tested and proven approaches are established for such activities as brand advertising, sales promotions, trade operations, specific aspects of consumer research, etc. Each approach is concerned with a 'key' part of the successful launching and managing of a brand. New recruits are passed through a planned training programme which exposes them to the experience the business has of the various approaches, and of the techniques and disciplines contained within them. Similar routines are carried out with personnel covering every section of the business.

In this way a trained and experienced group of managers is built up. They will be highly skilled in applying the 'knitting' – this is what they have been trained to do. And while the company 'sticks to the knitting' these managers are likely to be successful.

The important point is that under the systematic approach there will always be a number of people trained in the various business approaches employed by the company. New recruits will receive training in the 'company way' so that the approach will continue even if some of the trained managers leave or retire. The 'company way' will be part of the 'knitting'.

The use of the systematic approach acts to re-emphasize the need for the business to 'stick to the knitting' for it is in part of the 'knitting' that each of the managers and other employees have been trained. Should the company move into new markets and other new areas then the managers' ability will be suspect. It can be argued that the stronger the development of the 'knitting' within the training programmes and other development courses used in the business, the greater is the risk for the managers should they attempt to operate in entirely new fields.

The 'personal' approach hinges very much on the personal ability of a limited number of managers – normally a group of very senior people. It could be just one or two executives. These managers take all the 'key' decisions. In essence, they and their special ability represent the 'knitting' for the business.

Some of the best examples of the 'personal' approach at work can often be seen in professional partnerships. Here the 'knitting' is very much the special ability of the partners – the lawyer who has a highly developed knowledge of a part of the legal system, or the accountant who is highly skilled in, for instance, the workings of a special part of an international taxation agreement.

The 'personal' approach can also apply to industrial companies. Earlier the Hanson Company, a highly successful conglomerate, was mentioned. There has been considerable speculation as to whether the key decisions for Hanson's major operations are taken by the two founders of the business (Lord Hanson and Lord White) or whether they are shared by a much wider group of executives. Only those within Hanson at a senior level will know the answer. It is, of course, an answer of major significance to the company. If a 'personal' approach is employed and the two Lords do, in fact, take the key decisions, then their skill and ability represents the company's 'knitting'

Wherever the 'personal' approach applies, should anything happen to prevent the individual (or individuals) performing, then the business will no longer be able to practise its 'knitting'. Clearly this can be a consideration of major significance – it could be the beginning of the end of the business.

The 'Knitting' and Geographical Development

Can the 'knitting' of a business be limited by the district or country in which the company trades? The answer must be "Yes" if the knowledge and skills of the people concerned within the business are limited to a particular district or country.

The number of U.K. companies that have encountered difficulties as they have tried to progress in foreign markets is extensive. The problems encountered by some of the U.K. banks as they tried to become established in the U.S.A. are well known and well publicized.

One of the major difficulties companies invariably meet centres on their lack of the necessary detailed knowledge of the local markets and how best to trade within them. But U.K. companies are not alone in this. The same remarks apply to foreign companies investing in the U.K.

■ *If a company moves into a foreign market, even when it restricts its operations to those which have proven highly successful in its home market, if it does not take appropriate steps to ensure that it is fully equipped in all ways with the necessary local knowledge, then it will be moving 'outside of its knitting' and the risk will be that much higher.*

Stick to the 'Knitting' can Apply on a Geographical Basis

Federal Express is widely recognized as one of the outstanding business success stories in the U.S.A. The basic concept on which the company's business was built was skilfully conceived and developed. The strategic and operating management of the business was considered to be of a very high level. And yet when Federal Express tried to move its business into Europe it encountered extreme difficulties.

This is how the U.S. magazine *Newsweek*, in its edition for 30 March 1992, commented on the Federal Express move into Europe:

In only two decades, Federal Express went from nothing to a $7.7 billion, 380 plane company on a simple promise – that vital letters and parcels would reach their destination "absolutely, positively" overnight. Last week, however, after investing seven years and $2.5 billion overseas, the overnight pioneer said that Europe can wait. Punished by large losses – $193 million in the last quarter – the Tennessee-based courier announced it was all but rolling up its carpet in Europe. In May the company will stop deliveries between 109 European cities; after that, service will be limited to transatlantic deliveries between the United States and 16 major cities. Deliveries outside those cities will be subcontracted to other firms. European staff – now 9,200 – will shrink to 2,600.

What went wrong? The task of turning an incredibly successful American enterprise into a global operation proved to be too much. It's a bitter blow for FedEx chief and founder Frederick W. Smith, who conceived the idea for the overnight delivery industry while still in business school. "We thought that what worked in the States would work in Europe," says FedEx spokesman Dan Copp in Memphis. "That was a fallacy." As more and more U.S. firms aim for overseas markets – America's current account deficit dropped $1.4 billion during the last quarter, to $10.3 billion – the European crash of Federal Express holds tough lessons for American executives.

It is clear that an intimate knowledge of the market in which you trade, and of the conditions which apply within it, is part of the 'knitting'. The management of Federal Express have this knowledge in the U.S. market, but they did not have it in the European market. If you do not have an intimate knowledge of the market in which you intend to trade, and have not taken appropriate action to acquire this knowledge, then the move into the market is *not* 'knitting'.

Federal Express does not appear to have had a satisfactory knowledge of the European market into which it moved. The Federal Express move was *outside* of its 'knitting', and it suffered accordingly.

STICK TO THE 'KNITTING' has become probably the most widely quoted, and accepted, of the golden rules.

The record is very clear. If you want business success you are well advised to STICK TO THE 'KNITTING'. Furthermore, it is most important that you take the trouble to be sure you know just what your 'knitting' really is. A vague definition such as "to manufacture and market fast moving consumer products" is not good enough. Indeed, the acceptance of such a vague definition could well cause considerable trouble for your business.

Essentially your 'knitting' is that business operation, or series of operations, that you have demonstrated an ability to perform at a level of effectiveness which is superior to that of your competitors. It is an operation that you have the ability to repeat at the same standard.

Your knitting is closely aligned with the skill and ability of the people of your business, and in particular with the skill and ability of your management.

If you are ever tempted to move outside of your 'knitting' be sure your competitive advantage is a significant one, and one you can protect. It may be well worth your while to invest in a 'learning experience'.

Chapter 2

You Ignore the 'Best Value' Concept at Your Peril

to get and to keep customers
*you must provide them with what **they** believe is*
'best value'

This golden rule is probably the most basic, and in many respects, the simplest, of all the golden rules; but it must certainly rank as one of the most important.

To understand the rule it is, of course, necessary to appreciate the reasoning of the 'best value' concept. The 'best value' concept is based on the very simple fact that whenever a customer makes a purchase he always buys the particular brand or product which, at the time of purchase, represents 'best value' to him.

This applies to the woman buying detergent in the local supermarket, to the man buying a shirt in a local store, and to the industrialist buying a motor vehicle or a machine tool. It applies to all buyers; that is, it applies to all customers.

Anyone who wants to succeed in business needs to recognize the simple and fundamental reasoning of the 'best value' concept. To survive and prosper his business must, over time, make a profit. To realize a profit he must make sales. To make sales he must create and satisfy customers, and to do this it is essential that his brands or products represent 'best value' to a satisfactory number of people.

Many of the experienced strategy and operating practitioners will refer to this golden rule in such terms as "Always listen to your customers" or "Never argue with your customers, be sure to give them what they want". They are using their own form of shorthand for the 'best value' approach.

The 'best value' concept centres on the basic purpose of a business – to create and satisfy customers. It makes clear the vital importance of the customer, and the fact that at the time of purchase he makes the 'key' judgement decision as to which brand/product is 'best value'.

■ *A successful business achieves its objectives through the fulfilment of its purpose. It creates and satisfies customers by ensuring it provides 'best value', and it does this profitably.*

In effect this golden rule says "If you ignore your customers you will soon be in big, very big, trouble. You must make it your business to know what represents 'best value' to a satisfactory number of customers, and be sure your brand/product provides this to them on a continuing basis."

What is 'Best Value'?

Value is, of course, a subjective quality. For a particular brand it will differ from person to person and, for the individual person, from time to time. Small variations can be key value considerations for some people. Variations such as the colour of the package or the style of the print, which do not affect the performance of the product in any way, can make a material difference in value for a minority of people.

Numerous approaches have been developed for the valuation of a particular brand/product at a given time. Complex formulas have been proposed as the 'right' way for value assessment. In fact, there is no 'right' way. Value is judged by the individual and each individual has his own approach, and at times some of the approaches used may appear somewhat strange.

However, for the large majority of people more reasoned brand attributes are the key factors in value appreciation.

- Are there a series of *key* attributes which the majority of customers apply in making their *best value* decisions?

- If so, what are they?
- Can they be applied across all markets?

■ *These are tremendously important questions for any business operator. If he wants the customers' money – and he must have it if his business is to survive and prosper – he must provide best value to a satisfactory number of customers. Clearly he needs to have a thorough understanding, what might be termed as a 'sound feel', as to what represents 'best value' in his markets, and in particular best value to those consumers to whom his brand is primarily directed.*

The 'Best Value' Equation

Extensive and detailed research, backed by considerable practical experience, suggests there are certain key attributes which apply for a large majority of consumers, in a wide range of markets, when they make their value judgements. It is suggested that these attributes also apply in the industrial and service markets but there may be a difference in emphasis in their application.

The *key* attributes in the consumer *best value* equation are:

- Purpose.
- Performance.
- Price.
- Presentation.

PURPOSE

Purpose refers to the consumer need the brand meets, or the consumer benefit it provides. A brand/product that fails to meet the basic purpose for which the consumer has purchased it will clearly have only limited value for him. For example, a woman looking for a dress to wear to a formal social evening is unlikely to find a dress designed and made for beachwear a 'best value' buy on this occasion.

The same reasoning applies to the housewife as she makes her purchases. If she has a family which produces dirty shirts, sheets, and so on, then she will have a need for a brand/product which meets her requirement to clean them. To have value to her the washing powder must meet this basic purpose.

As people become more prosperous and sophisticated their requirements develop and their needs tend to broaden. Thus, the washing powder may need to 'clean, whiten, and soften' and a toilet soap may need to 'clean and deodorize'. The growth of these various additional consumer requirements is, in effect, the development of a form of segmentation within the market.

The link between a brand's 'purpose' and its 'promise' requires explanation. The brand's 'purpose' is the consumer need it meets, or benefit it provides, expressed in manufacturer's terms. The terms could be of a technical nature and not necessarily be understood by the consumer. The brand's 'promise' is its 'purpose' expressed in terms that are understood, accepted, and appreciated by the consumer. For instance, for a washing powder brand, such as *Persil*, the purpose could have been stated in technical terms which relate to how the product removes dirt and stains from soiled sheets, shirts etc., and returns them to their original colour. The *Persil* promise states very simply 'Persil Washes Whiter'.

The brand's promise is invariably a very important factor within its advertising. It takes considerable skill to define and express a brand promise in the right words and manner. The consumer must understand, appreciate, and accept it. For instance, at one time in the U.K. it was thought to be important that a washing powder's promise should be expressed as getting clothes white rather than clean. The consumer believed that whiteness was more totally embracing than cleanness. This was at a time when much of the wash was, in fact, made up of predominantly white items.

There is also a skill in discovering a consumer need that is not adequately met by existing brands. Consumers frequently have difficulty in defining their requirements with clarity. Knowing how to structure and conduct a consumer research exercise which will open up the consumer's thinking, and enable him to state his need more precisely, can provide the base for a valuable marketing opportunity.

■ *The basic fact is that to have a value to the consumer a brand must meet his need or requirement. It must promise and deliver the benefit for which it is purchased.*

PERFORMANCE

A brand's value is markedly influenced by how well it performs in meeting the purpose.

Many brands may have the same or a similar purpose, but they are unlikely to have the same performance. The manufacturer's skill in product formulation, in processing, and in the quality of the ingredients he is prepared to use, can all be significant factors in the way the brand performs.

In a brand's value equation the performance rating which really matters is that given to it by consumers, and this will not necessarily be the same as that shown in the manufacturer's laboratory. Specific ingredients which have advanced technological properties, but which do not show through to the consumer in results, are unlikely to affect performance appreciation and in turn the consumer view of brand value.

In practice, consumers often have their own personal approach to performance rating. For instance, they may judge their washing powder when they have a particular kind of wash, possibly one where the clothes are heavily soiled. Others may make their judgement only when they wash in high temperature water, and so on. It is an important part of the skill of a manufacturer to know the ways in which consumers judge performance, and to formulate his brand accordingly.

Frequently there will be a need to get from the consumer a comparative rating of performance. In the market-place battle the brand requirement is often to obtain not just a better, but a significantly better, performance. If the rating of the brand is only marginally better it may not be worth a major exploitation effort. But a significant improvement, one that the consumer recognizes readily, could be a very different proposition and warrant substantial backing. The ability to research consumers' perceptions and to form an accurate view of comparative performance ratings is a valuable skill.

■ *Performance is clearly a vitally important factor in a brand's value equation. The wise manufacturer never underestimates the consumer's ability to make a sound judgement of a brand's performance. There is considerable evidence, from many product categories, to show that over time the consumer is invariably a very sound judge of brand performance.*

PRICE

It is an elementary fact that the money the consumer pays for a brand is its price. Money is a measure, and so price is very much part of the value equation.

Given two brands with the same purpose and the same level of performance, the one with the lower price would get the consumer's vote as the best value. (This ignores the value of brand presentation which could affect the buying decision and is considered below.)

The price in the value equation is always the one which applies on the particular occasion when the buying decision is made. This means that if a brand is enjoying a special price reduction in a store, it is more likely to attract the consumer's custom because its value has been improved. At the lower price level it is more likely to be rated as best value. Similarly, if a special pack containing an extra quantity of product is offered without an increase in price, the value of the brand will rise and its prospects of being considered as best value improved.

As with brand performance, skill in judging what level of price differential the consumer considers significant is important:

- What level of differential will motivate him to change his buying decision?
- Would a move of 1p per unit make any worthwhile difference to competitive value?
- Or is 5p per unit the minimum adjustment required to make an impact and get a buying decision change?

In theory, with the help of a suitably planned series of tests, it should be relatively easy to plot the movement of brand demand with varying levels of price adjustment. Useful guidelines should be obtainable from the research; however, in the real market-place, competitive prices and market conditions rarely remain static, so making an exact plot of price movement is unlikely to be possible.

The manufacturer needs reliable information that will help him decide what is the most favourable price position for his brand compared with other brands in the market, accepting that his ultimate objective will be to make a satisfactory level of both sales and profit. He will need to have a 'sound feel' for the price dynamics of his market.

He also needs a sound 'feel' for the relationship between performance and price. When he has clarified and settled on his brand purpose, it is with the attributes of performance and price that he will be primarily concerned in any attempts he may make to change his brand value to his customers.

Of course, the consumer's reaction to price can often be affected by the movement of his income. Given a liberal supply of funds the customer is more likely to place a higher weighting on performance and a lower one on price. However, this is certainly not to say that the purchase of lower priced brands is necessarily concentrated with the lower income groups.

■ *Of the key attributes in the brand value equation, price is the one which can be moved most rapidly. A change in other attributes invariably requires considerable time in preparation. This has tended to mean that price is often reasoned to be a short-term operational 'tool'. Price is an important factor within operations, but it can also be a vitally important factor within business strategy.*

PRESENTATION

In presenting his brand the manufacturer should be concerned to inform his prospective customer of the brand's purpose, its performance and – as appropriate – its price. The presentation will have as one of its main objectives the task of getting the consumer to try the brand and, in the case of regular users, of ensuring re-trial. One of the best ways of convincing consumers that a brand offers best value is to get them to try it. Only in use can they really judge the brand's performance standard.

It should always be remembered that there are only two ways in which the sales volume of a brand can increase. One is by increased penetration, which means increased trial. The other is by persuading existing users to increase their consumption. Getting consumer trial is fundamental to ultimate success.

No matter how he sets about the task of presenting his brand, no matter what style, manner, or setting he chooses, the manufacturer is bound to make a brand impression. The package can be designed with loud, gaudy colours, or with soft, gentle colours. The style of the presentation can be noisy and aggressive, or it can be quiet and unassuming. The manufacturer must decide which approach he wishes to use.

The presentation will automatically help to build a brand personality or, as it is sometimes termed, a brand image. It is clearly better to build a personality which is helpful to the progress of the brand rather than one that is damaging. This means that the manufacturer should decide on the type, style, and form of personality he wants for his brand. He should decide this well before he enters the market, and he should then ensure that his brand presentations work to develop and maintain that personality.

■ *There is no good reason why a skilfully formed presentation should not fulfil the double requirement – it should do an outstanding selling job, encouraging the consumer to try and re-try the brand, and it should do this in a style which plays its full part in helping to build the desired brand personality.*

There is considerable evidence to show that where a brand has built the right personality this can have a beneficial effect on its value, and it can be a helpful factor in enabling it to pass the consumer's best value test.

Synergy of the 'Best Value' Attributes

There is undoubtedly a synergy between the best value attributes in practice. The record shows that for real success a brand needs to have the right purpose, the right balance between performance and price, the right presentation, and to allow the attributes to work in support of each other and for the brand.

The right purpose is directly linked to the consumer need in the market, or market section, at which the brand is directed. With the balance of performance and price, a high level performance (i.e. high when compared with other brands in the market) can normally command a higher level of price, whereas a lower level of performance would normally need a lower price.

A strong and favourable personality is unlikely to bring a brand success if the purpose is wrong, or if the balance between performance and price is badly aligned. However, a favourable personality will most certainly be helpful to the brand and may cover, to some extent, an imbalance between performance and price.

In competitive positions where a number of brands have very similar purposes, and also a similar level of performance and price, then the brand personality will be a 'key' consideration in deciding the consumer's choice of 'best value'.

■ *The basic fact which is worthy of repetition is that when all the brand's key value attributes are 'right' they will build on each other, and this will act to increase their total value.*

Persil and the 'Best Value' Concept

Great brands invariably conform with the 'best value' concept. They have the right purpose for the market sector at which they are primarily directed, they have the right balance between performance and price, and they have ensured that their presentation is effective both in encouraging trial and re-trial, and also in developing the right brand personality.

Persil must rate as one of the greatest successes in brand marketing in U.K. history. Its major development period was through the 1950s and 60s, and it has been strong enough to remain a great brand through the 1970s, 80s, and into the 1990s.

Through three decades into the 1970s *Persil* lead the highly competitive U.K. washing powder market. It was strong enough to withstand almost continuous attack from the synthetic detergents. Its position of leadership was lost only when the composition of the total market changed from purely high sudsing powders to a mixture of high and low sudsing products. *Persil* is a high sudsing powder – *Persil Automatic* is a low sudsing powder and took over the total market leadership position from *Persil* in the late 1970s.

The *Persil* success is often attributed to its advertising. It has certainly been supported by very skilful advertising, particularly during its leadership period. However, closer examination shows that *Persil*, throughout its highly successful leadership period, conformed very closely to the best value approach.

Persil's purpose was concerned with the provision of superior whiteness – the brand's promise was 'Persil Washes Whiter'. This was clearly the right benefit for a main sector product at a time when most of a typical household's wash was in fact white. Beyond this, the benefit of whiteness was believed to have a higher overall value to the housewife than, for instance, cleanness.

The *Persil* formulation was an especially effective one, providing a very high level of performance. *Persil* contained a large quantity of soap which is known to be a most efficient detergent and also a relatively high level of perborate. Perborate is a particularly effective ingredient in removing stains when used in a high temperature wash. Through the 1950s and 60s it was very common for the housewife to do her wash in very hot, often boiling, water.

Persil also packed a slightly higher weight of powder in its packets (thereby encouraging heavier use) than did its major competitors.

Persil prices were normally below the price levels of the competitive synthetic detergent brands.

To a very strong position in purpose, performance and price *Persil* added highly competent presentation – the *Persil* personality was extremely well developed and clearly very 'right' for the brand. Little wonder, then, that *Persil* should have been such a great success and have represented best value to so many people buying washing powders in the U.K. during the 1950s and 60s.

Never Underestimate the Customer

This statement, or one very close to it, will be heard frequently by the young manager as he works his way up the business management ladder. The 'older hands' will raise it often and in particular when he proposes a major change, for instance, in formula, in pack design, in pricing, or in brand advertising.

In some cases the statement will be worded as "Stay close to your customer". This is where the term 'listen' is often employed, as in "Always *listen* to your customer". The exact wording is not the important consideration. What is important is the basic thought behind the statement. The customer is all important – without customers there is no business.

■ *The statement is a form of reinforcement of the 'best value' concept and will often be used in this way. The concept also concentrates on the customer, and reasons that it is the customer's view as to what is the 'best value' that is all important. This view may differ from that of the highly trained and well-qualified chemist who designed the original formula, or the production man who manufactures the product so effectively, or the marketing manager who orchestrated the marketing research and helped formulate the advertising. In the final analysis it is the valuation of the customer which really matters.*

Of course this brings to the fore a number of 'key' questions such as "Who is your customer?", "Who are the potential customers?" and "How do these existing and potential customers decide what is 'best value'?" "What are the important value considerations to them?"

WHO IS THE CUSTOMER?

The very simple answer is "the individual who actually purchases the brand/product". This is, of course, correct and means that in some cases the manufacturer actually knows personally each one of his customers. In instances such as this there is most certainly no excuse for not 'listening' to the customer, or in any way underestimating him.

There are many companies where the list of customers is very limited. Included among such businesses are many of the smaller operators who service specialized market sectors – they may not know every customer personally but they do have a close knowledge of who they are, where and how they do business, and what they expect from the brand/product supplied. However, there are many businesses that have no direct business contact with their 'ultimate' customer. They sell to wholesalers and multiple chains who in turn sell on to the 'ultimate' customer.

The remarks about never underestimating the customer certainly apply to the wholesaler and similar traders, but they are really directed to the 'ultimate' customers (i.e. the consumers).

The fact is that there are many manufacturers who have very little knowledge as to just who their ultimate customers are. It is very difficult to listen to people, or to stay close to them, if you don't know who they are.

And so the first requirement is to find out just who your customers are. The structure of the customer base for each brand/product will tend to vary depending on its type and form. Frequently it will be possible to classify customers in terms of consumption (e.g. very heavy, medium, and light). This form of classification can be of great consequence. It may be that a relatively small number of customers account for a very large part of total consumption, and the big majority of consumers are in fact light consumers who account for a relatively small part of total consumption. All customers are important, although some are just that little more important than others!

The 'best value' concept points out that customers always purchase the brand/product that, at the time of purchase, represents to them 'best value'.

It follows that the vitally important factor behind the requirement to know your customers centres on the need to be able to verify just why your brand/product represents 'best value' to them, and, beyond this, to know of their likes and dislikes of the brand so that these may be accommodated, as appropriate, into the future.

■ *Of course, not all the customers will have the same reasons for their 'best value' decision. Some may be impressed with the brand's performance, others with its price, and some may be influenced by the brand presentation. But only if you take the trouble to find out who your customers are can you begin to appreciate their views and use this knowledge to strengthen your brand's position.*

POTENTIAL CUSTOMERS

"The customers you have are worth much more than those you *might* have sometime in the future." This is another of the statements that is often made when new developments in brand formulation, packaging, etc. are up for discussion. It contains a form of warning which is worthy of full consideration.

In normal circumstances the customers you have are worth more than your potential customers for the simple reason that the potentials may never become actual customers. The potentials may never vote your brand 'best value' with their money.

The danger is that in attempting to attract new buyers the manufacturer may be tempted to adjust, for instance, his brand formulation, his packaging, or possibly his advertising promise. This may well help to attract the 'potentials' but it could offend his 'regulars'. And if the 'regulars' leave and the 'potentials' fail to materialize then the manufacturer could have real trouble.

■ *As a general rule, all brand adjustments should be checked for approval with regular buyers first, and then when their approval is registered, the adjustments should move forward for the approval of the potential new buyers. The aim should be a new formulation, or whatever the adjustment is, that is fully approved as 'best value' by the regulars and which is also attractive to the potential new customers. A research study that fails to differentiate between the two categories could be dangerous.*

Of course there may be an occasion when a brand decides as a deliberate act of policy to go out to attract a new category of customer and it may be fully prepared to lose its current group of regular customers.

The important requirement is that this action should be taken only after full consideration of the brand's position and its prospects for the future should the adjustments mean it fails to remain 'best value' for its established buyers. For instance, if the quality of a brand is increased markedly and an upward price adjustment is considered necessary to cover the move. Many of the regulars may object to the price increase. The position may be an acceptable one if the potential new buyers attracted by the development become 'regulars'. But the manufacturer will need to be as sure as is possible that his adjustments are 'right' and that the potential buyers are going to become actual buyers.

UNDERESTIMATING THE CUSTOMER

This phrase is normally used with reference to the customer's appreciation of value. Frequently the specialists within the manufacturer's staff are either unable of unwilling to credit the customer with the ability to come to his own decision as to what represents 'best value'. If they are concerned with the brand's formulation then they find it difficult to accept that the consumer may differ from their view as to the level of performance produced. They may believe that a certain ingredient provides a benefit of considerable value, but then discover that the consumer disagrees and is prepared to ignore the particular ingredient, and so on.

Sometimes the difference for the customer may relate to the brand's price. The manufacturer's staff may believe a popular price should be 50p per unit. But the consumer refuses to pay 50p and looks for a lower unit price.

Advertising is an area where problems often arise under this heading. The rather 'clever' advertisement, deeply admired by other advertising professionals, fails to impress the consumer. He does not accept the brand demonstration, and fails to go out and try the brand.

Sometimes the problem is that the customer does react favourably to the brand advertising, but then rejects the brand as not meeting the standard as portrayed in the advertisement.

■ *The experienced and skilled operator never underestimates the customer. He never attempts to be unduly 'clever' in his approach. He never attempts to lecture the customer. And he most certainly would never attempt to mislead the customer. In fact, he always treats the customer with the utmost respect.*

Value and Quality

"For the longer term, we believe it is important that our brands compete in the quality sector of the market." "We set out to built quality into all our brands." "There is no future for brands that rely on price, we believe in building in quality."

These, and similar statements, are often made by business leaders.

marketing directors, advertising specialists, and others closely linked with the marketing of a particular brand or group of brands. They often go on to add that they are intent on "building value into their brands". Another area often mentioned is service. For companies selling complex machinery where the customer is looking for a service assurance, to build it in at a higher level is often referred to as "adding quality and value".

There is a need to be sure what is meant by the terms 'value' and 'quality'. They are often used as if they are synonymous; but they are not synonymous and the difference between them is important. The *Oxford English Dictionary* talks of 'quality' as a degree of excellence, while of 'value' it talks of worth. The 'best value' concept recognizes this difference in that price, a monetary expression of worth, is an important consideration within the concept. Quality is not mentioned directly in the concept; however, it is, of course, a significant factor within performance and is recognized in this way.

The quality of a brand or product may be improved by:

1. More effective use of the existing brand formula and/or design; or
2. A deliberate input of additional ingredients and/or design.

The difference between the two approaches is of consequence. A more effective use of the existing formula will not involve any additional cost, and it could bring a reduction. The input of additional ingredients will mean an increase of costs.

During the 1960s and 70s many of the motor cars imported into the U.K., in particular those from Japan, were thought to be of a higher quality than many of the cars produced in the U.K. The Japanese cars did not necessarily have superior mechanisms but they were thought to have been assembled with greater care and attention. In fact it was probably less costly to carry out the higher 'quality' assembly as expensive correction and repairs were avoided.

Clearly this form of quality improvement should be pursued aggressively by management. If brand quality is improved and price is unchanged then brand value will rise. And this rise in value will have been achieved without any increase in cost.

When the approach of using an additional ingredient or design is used a degree of extra cost will be incurred. If price is unchanged then value will rise, but brand unit margin will fall.

When executives talk of "building in value" what they usually mean is taking the brand up-market. They are prepared to accept a higher unit cost to give the brand some form of 'extra' with the customer, and for this they will ask a higher price. Through recent years the rapid development of distributor or 'own-label' brands has encouraged many manufacturers to follow this 'up-market' approach.

Of course, the approach can be overdone if it means an unduly high price. Price is also a factor within the 'best value' concept and the requirement is to keep the 'right' balance of performance and price for the particular customers to whom the brand is primarily directed.

■ *It is worth repeating that the improvement of performance – that is, an improvement in quality without an increase in cost – is the approach that should be vigorously pursued by management. Of course, the real objective should be to improve performance and reduce cost – not easily achieved, but often possible with a positive and innovative approach.*

Knowing What is 'Best Value' for Your Customers

One of the reasons why the golden rule STICK TO THE KNITTING has proved so 'right' is that, over time, good operators build up an exceptional knowledge of the areas in which they specialize. This applies particularly to the operator's understanding of what represents 'best value' in the markets, and especially in the market segments, in which he competes.

The operator who concentrates on the production and marketing of, for instance, deodorant soap should, over time, build up a very specialized knowledge as to how much his customers are prepared to pay for various kinds and levels of deodorancy, and beyond this how many people are likely to be interested in this form and type of brand. Similar remarks will apply to almost all markets, and market segments.

The need for the operator to have a 'sound feel' as to what represents 'best value' in his markets, and in particular 'best value' to those consumers to whom his brand is primarily directed, has already been emphasized.

Of course, it will be argued that skilful marketing research will provide answers to many of the 'best value' questions. Skilful marketing research will provide guidance, but good judgement will be vitally important.

Criticism of the 'Best Value' Apporach

A comment often heard when the 'best value' concept is discussed is that it does not sufficiently acknowledge the power of advertising. For instance: Brand A and Brand B are known to have almost identical formulations with equal performance. Brand A is heavily advertised while Brand B has very little advertising. Brand A is stocked widely while Brand B has limited store distribution. Brand A sells at 50p per 10oz packet and Brand B sells at 40p for a similar packet. Brand A outsells Brand B by 3 to 1.

The argument is that this is surely a wrong evaluation of the respective brands caused by advertising. Brand A is said to have a 'perceived value' (as against a real value) that is superior to that of Brand B.

If the consumers of the two brands are paying the prices quoted in a free and competitive market situation, and they are using their own money, then those who buy Brand A at 50p clearly believe it to be 'best value', and those who buy Brand B at 40p consider B to be 'best value'. There is no difference between the so termed 'perceived value' and 'real value'.

It is important to examine why a position of this kind arises. The following points are of significance:

1. *How many of the people concerned have actually tried both Brand A and Brand B?*
   It is only when the consumer actually tries the brand for himself that he can really make a judgement on its performance and, in turn, on its value.

2. *The store distribution of Brand B is stated to be much more limited than that for Brand A.*

   The lack of store distribution will be a key factor in limiting the trial of Brand B. However, beyond this it will mean that in many stores those consumers who have been able to try Brand B, and possibly consider it 'best value', will not be able to buy it. Brand A is readily available.

3. *We do not know the standard of presentation, in particular their packaging, employed by the brands.*

   A well-designed, and properly structured, package can be of considerable importance. If Brand A has good, well-designed packaging, and Brand B's packaging is at a poor level, then this could have a material influence on the buying decision of many consumers.

4. *If the heavier advertising of Brand A is good advertising, then it will encourage potential consumers to try the brand, it will encourage existing consumers to continue using the brand, and it will help to build a favourable brand personality. After all, this is what good advertising should do.*

   Given that Brand A's advertising is good, then the considerably heavier level of investment behind it must be helpful to the brand.

   This will be of particular importance if the market is in its growth stage with many new consumers joining it.

   Many of these new consumers will know only of Brand A, and it will be the only brand they are able to buy in their local store.

However, in cases such as the one illustrated, the importance of the heavier advertising should not be overrated. Brand B's problem is much more likely to be centred on the two basic considerations:

1. Lack of trial; and
2. Lack of store distribution.

If Brand B has decided against using extensive advertising, then it must develop other approaches to encourage consumer trial. There are other approaches available and in many cases they can prove more effective than advertising. Beyond this it will need to work on its store distribution problem. Even if the brand did have strong advertising, much of it would be wasted without a satisfactory store distribution.

It is worth noting that over recent periods many distributor brands (also known as own label) have become market leaders within their own particular store chain. Such brands rarely have direct advertising support, but, of course, they do have full distribution and feature within their own stores.

The brand advertising, and the brand personality it helps to build, tends to be particularly important in markets where the buyer behaviour is classified as 'very emotional'. A market often quoted as a good example of the 'emotional buy' is that for perfume. Presentation, in its widest sense, is clearly of great significance in the sale of packaged perfumes.

The use of advertising to obtain brand trial and re-trial is normally accepted. The objections tend to centre on the development of the brand personality and the idea that it can represent a false value.

It should be appreciated that when a manufacturer gives his brand any form of publicity, whether it be television advertising, showcards placed in a store, or a particular form of pack design, he is sure to create an impression. Clearly it is very desirable that the impression he creates should be favourable rather than unfavourable. However, it is important that this 'personality value' should not be overrated. If a brand's purpose is unsound, or its balance between performance and price badly out of alignment, then the most favourable of personalities is unlikely to rescue it.

■ *With well-established brands the favourable personality factor can make a difference, but it is usually of a more marginal nature. It may enable a leading brand to take a small premium, but it is very unlikely to allow a premium of 25% as shown in the illustration above. When differences of this kind apply and the product performance is equal, certain basic considerations (such as lack of trial, and/or distribution) are invariably involved.*

'Best Value' and Profit

It is, of course, relatively simple to make a brand/product 'best value' and lose money in large quantities. Price is part of the value equation and if you reduce it the value of the brand/product will rise. If the price is reduced enough the brand should become 'best value' to more and more customers – but the losses could also grow.

The requirement for a successful business is that the purpose should be fulfilled and the objective achieved. One of the foremost reasons for business failures is that managers, in their haste to meet the 'best value' requirement, forget, or misjudge in some way, the need to make profit.

To both meet the purpose and achieve the objective is the big challenge for business managers. And the challenge is not just for one occasion, or for one year – the challenge is on a continuous basis. In the final analysis, this is what business strategy and operations are all about – fulfilling purpose and achieving objective.

■ *The fact that it is necessary to make profit does not, in any way, reduce the need to ensure that the brand/product becomes 'best value' for a satisfactory number of consumers. If you cannot meet the business purpose there is no prospect whatsoever that you will achieve your profit objective.*

The 'Best Value' Concept in Strategy and Operations

The objective of business strategy and operations is to build a successful business. To be successful a business will need to have one or more successful brands.

The record shows that successful brands invariably have the 'right' purpose, the 'right' balance between performance and price, and to this they add the 'right' presentation. Successful brands comply with the approach of the 'best value' concept.

The fact that a brand complies with the approach will not guarantee success. It will need to be managed with a satisfactory level of skill and enthusiasm, and backed by sufficient resources. However, if a brand disregards the 'best value' concept, then even if it is skilfully operated and has the necessary resources, it is unlikely to be successful.

One of the great dangers in strategy formulation is that a detailed plan will be based, for instance, on the launch of a series of brands which are to command a price premium in the market. But if the required performance level fails to materialize and a price premium is not possible, the detailed strategic plan will be in disarray.

Frequently, within strategic plans far too much is required of brand presentation. It is required to do much more than its basic job of gaining brand trial and re-trial – it is expected to build a brand personality that will justify a substantial price premium, and to do this without any worthwhile performance plus. Plans of this kind usually fail.

The purpose proposed for a new brand is always of marked significance. To some considerable extent it positions the brand within its market and materially affects its volume potential. There is a requirement to be as sure as is possible that the brand will have the ability to deliver the purpose. Without delivery the brand is unlikely to make any progress.

Pricing is a further area where problems can frequently arise. As markets develop unit prices within the market tend to fall. The balance between performance and price tends to move towards price and the attractive unit margins disappear. If the brand attempts to hold its old price (i.e. pre-market development) it is unlikely to prove 'best value' to many customers. The strategy needs to appreciate this.

The consideration of the 'best value' concept is particularly important for new brands, and new brands frequently feature prominently within strategic plans. To challenge an established brand market leader without a significant competitive advantage in purpose, performance, or price is likely to prove an expensive and unsuccessful exercise. The 'best value' concept warns against such exercises. The challenger must produce more than 'equal value', he must produce 'better value' and for this his superiority will need to be more than marginal.

Wherever the 'best value' concept is accepted and applied within the strategic and operational planning process the resulting plan should at least be realistic in allowing for the vitally important contribution of the *customer,* and of the fact that it is the customer's decision as to what is 'best value' that is all important. The major misjudgments which are often present when a technical or an advertising/sales view is allowed to dominate the brand review need to be avoided.

At the present time one of the outstanding developments in the consumer goods markets in the U.K., U.S.A., and in other developed countries, is the rise of the distributor brands (brands owned and controlled by retailers, also known as 'own label'). These brands have become 'best value' to a growing sector of the population. Often the problem for the manufacturers' brands would appear to be that they have allowed their balance between performance and price to get out of alignment – they are expecting the customer to pay too much for what are often relatively small differences in performance. Frequently they are expecting their presentation to make a large contribution to brand value. The experienced operator will know that to rely on presentation to generate a considerable part of brand value is a high risk approach; the 'best value' concept warns against it.

The basic point is that the 'best value' concept, and the reasoning behind it, are backed by considerable market-place experience. The concept is simple in approach, and in many respects can be considered good business common sense. Plans contained within the business strategy, and within operations, which disregard the reasoning of the 'best value' approach should be questioned very closely. They may, for special reasons, bring business success; but if you ignore the concept you are much more likely to meet trouble.

■ *This golden rule is all about how you relate to, and how you treat, your customers.*

Without customers there is no business. The customer contributes the revenue which goes to pay the staff, the suppliers, all the other expenses of running the business, and the dividends. Customers are vitally important. To get them, and retain them, you have to give them what they believe to be 'best value'.

Customers deserve to be treated with every respect. They are worthy of great care and consideration. You ignore the customer at your peril, because it is the customer who makes the all important value judgement as to whether or not your brand is 'best value'. That is the very simple, yet so vitally important, message of this golden rule.

Chapter 3

Be 'First', Be 'Right'

and have 'surprise' on your side

Be First

The business which is first with a new product, a new promotion, a new form of packaging, or any other innovation, has an outstanding opportunity to establish a lead in the particular field. The business will have the opportunity to set the standard against which all other entrants to the field will be measured. Most importantly, the brand that is first has the opportunity to make its name synonymous with the provision of the particular benefit it provides.

When a consumer experiences a particular benefit for the first time, it is invariably a memorable occasion. The brand associated with the first experience has a clear opportunity to make a strong and lasting impression. It can also set the price structure for the market or sector concerned.

The brand that is first with the new development has the opportunity to become the leader in its particular market, or market sector, and to claim the advantages that go with leadership. These advantages should be extensive and include a lower unit cost for both production and distribution.

If you are first you should be able to consolidate your position, and in this way protect yourself from competitive attack.

In the longer term, the brand that is first should establish a firm leadership and be positioned to earn a higher level of profit than its competitors.

■ *The message is clear – be first.*

Be Right

It all seems very simple. The advantages which go with being first are so outstanding that there would surely be very little argument. But there is a limitation and it is of real consequence. It is that you should 'be first *and* be right'.

If you are first and you get it wrong then you would probably have been better off to have been second, or not to have competed at all. Beyond this you may well have helped your competitors by showing them what *not* to do. They will be able to read your market experience, they will know where and why you have failed, and they will be able to avoid making the same mistakes.

The ideal must be that your move is 'right' both strategically and operationally. If you are basically wrong strategically then your project is likely to be a failure even if you are right operationally. Should you be right strategically but have a poor operational performance then you may make some progress and in time be able to correct your operational mistakes. If you are very badly wrong operationally the probability is that you will fail even though you may be basically right strategically.

The strategic considerations will include the need to be moving into the right market, at the right time, and with a brand that has the right purpose (i.e. consumer benefit), the right performance/price balance, and the right presentation. These are fundamental considerations for a new brand. When the move is a major re-launch for an existing brand the need to get the right positions on such factors as purpose, performance, price, and presentation will apply in the same way as for a new brand.

The operational considerations will be concerned with the practical tasks involved in bringing into existence a brand which measures up to the strategic requirements, and then ensuring it makes satisfactory progress in the market place.

■ *Again the message is clear – be first, and be right.*

In the opening part of this chapter the consideration is with the golden rule BE 'FIRST', BE 'RIGHT'. However, the operator who wants an outstanding success should add a further factor, and one that many would argue is as important as being first – this additional factor is 'surprise'.

The second part of this chapter considers 'surprise'. Be 'first', be 'right', and add 'surprise' – these three factors add up to a golden rule of major significance. If your project can meet each one then it should most certainly be well on the road to success.

Getting There 'First' and 'Right'

In the real live world of business getting there both 'first' and 'right' is rarely a simple matter. There will be occasions when a manufacturer is able to develop a new product and then by the use of a strong patent provide it with very secure protection. He can then take time to conduct the various researches and tests to ensure he 'gets it right'. His protection will work to give him that valuable commodity – 'time'.

Positions of this sort appear occasionally, but they are the exception rather than the general rule. In by far the majority of cases the manufacturer will need to move rapidly. His competitors are likely to have similar views to his own in the field of product development, and he will be unable to obtain any strong patent or other protection for his product.

Normally the manufacturer's ability to take the new innovation through its product development, manufacture, and marketing, rapidly and faster than his competitors, will be vitally important if the brand is to be 'first'.

At one time it was customary to launch a new brand (or other innovative development) into a small test area and to keep it there for a reasonable period of time, possibly as long as 12 months, before moving it into the wider market.

The investment required to take the project into the wider market would be an extensive one – a lengthy test market was considered worth while to ensure the project was 'right'. There was always the risk that a competitor would jump in with a more extensive operation before the test area results were complete – but it was considered as a limited risk and one worth taking.

The process was a major consumer of time. Research and development time preparing the product, time preparing processing facilities, time preparing the marketing approach, and time to collect the results and to read them. The reading would normally require initial and repeat purchasing details. Time was a very important factor in the whole process.

The process could not guarantee success. Frequently the test market would be a failure, or part failure. Then more time could be required to correct mistakes and prepare for a further test.

Clearly this whole procedure could be very expensive in terms of both money and other resources. Through recent years there have been many developments in this field of activity and extended area test markets are no longer the general rule. Marketing researchers have worked hard to develop techniques which render these lengthy tests in the market unnecessary.

There are now a number of new testing techniques, each one strongly recommended by its supporters. Often they can be carried out in consumers' homes, or in special testing facilities, and in this respect they have a major plus over the market tests in that they are unlikely to be observed by competitors. But they still cannot guarantee success; their conclusions can be suspect.

The manufacturer must always expect to be involved in a trade off between his desire to be 'first' (which will require speed of action) and the risk he is prepared to take with his project proposition in terms of being 'right' (which may require time).

The important question he may need to ask, and answer, is "Just what degree of 'rightness' is it essential I obtain before I make my major move?"

The issue as to how much time the manufacturer can take and still be sure of being 'first' is a fundamental one. It can be argued that it is better to be first and 'mainly right' rather than second and 'right'. So much will depend on the definition given to 'mainly right'.

■ *Clearly the big prizes are likely to be reserved for those who are both 'first' **and** 'right'. To achieve this in a competitive environment two factors will be essential.*

The first of these is a high degree of effectiveness in operation. The requirement will encompass every section of the business from research and development through to the sales force. The business will need people who are highly skilled in their particular part of the operation, and a top management that can 'bring it all together' and ensure it is operated in the market both effectively and enthusiastically.

The second requirement will centre on a high quality of management judgement. It is most unlikely that sufficient time will be available to test all the 'key' considerations – management judgement will need to apply, and it had better be good, and that means 'right'.

Being 'Right': A Total Business Requirement

The need to be 'right' in terms of the make-up of the project (be it a brand or some other form of innovation) in the market has been stressed. It is important to appreciate that the requirement applies to the total company.

A highly successful brand launch will require additional funds to finance its production and distribution. If the funds are not available in sufficient quantity, and at the required time, then the operation could fail, even with an outstanding launch success. Similarly if the brand is successful but production facilities are unable to meet the demand then a well-equipped competitor could possibly move in and take over the unsatisfied customers and with them the market position.

For the brand to be 'right' under this heading it must be able to meet a business plan which is a sensible one for the operator. A plan that can cope with success, a plan that will not place him in a position where his backup resources are inadequate.

When Not to be 'First'

Is it possible there could be occasions when it is wise *not* to be first? As the golden rule makes clear, in the main, it is always advantageous to be first, but there can be special occasions when it may be advisable to be second or even later.

If you are the big operator in a market and you are considering an operation that is a high risk then it could possibly be advantageous for you to let one of your smaller competitors take the lead with the proposition. He will test the market for you, and he will take the major risk. If it fails then you will be saved all the problems that go with failure.

If the proposition succeeds then you should be able to make a rapid entrance to the market with a similar (hopefully a better) brand of your own and overpower the smaller opposition. You will probably need to back your entry with a much higher level of advertising and other marketing investment. You may need to use price to help you over the shorter term. Your stronger sales force and greater influence with the trade should also help.

Of course, there is the risk that the small competitor may get well established before you are able to mount your main attack, and it may prove impossible to overtake him. You could find yourself sharing the market or even as a junior member. The small man may sell his business to a larger organization with the finance to consolidate and then build on the potential which has been established, and then you could have a real threat.

These are among the risks you may have to accept if you allow a competitor to be 'first'. There is obviously a need to know your competitors, to know their capabilities, to be sure of their finances, and the strength and resolution of their management.

When a small business is in a position to be 'first' with a new development in what promises to be a major new market it could, in certain circumstances, be wise for it to allow one of its bigger competitors to take the lead. The initial marketing development investment is likely to be very heavy, and a considerable part could be in the form of consumer education. This could prove to be too much for the smaller company. If he allows his bigger competitor to carry this market development expense, and then when the market is of reasonable size, makes an entry with a specialist niche brand, the smaller operator will probably enjoy better financial success.

When a manufacturer is fully confident that he will have a new development available within a short time period, and this development will give him a significant competitive advantage, then he is probably well advised not to rush into the market but to wait for the new development.

In circumstances of this kind much will depend on:

1. Just how firm is the operator's confidence in having the new development available,
2. What is meant by a short time period, and
3. Just how significant a competitive advantage the new development will provide.

A new product development – for instance, a new formula that is expected to provide a significant performance advance – can illustrate the consideration the manufacturer may need to apply. His research and development managers may feel very confident they can deliver the new development, and they may be first class scientists who will not spare themselves. And yet every experienced executive knows that until the new product has proved itself in the appropriate tests, and his production personnel have shown they can process it satisfactorily, there is a degree of risk as to whether or not the new development will ever perform.

Again sound management judgement will be essential. The chief executive will know of the progress already made on the project when he needs to take his decision, and he will know his personnel working on the project. He will know whether they are by nature optimists or pessimists – and this is important, for a borderline decision may well hinge on his view of his colleagues outlook.

Obviously the time period of the delay in producing the new development is of consequence. Six months may be acceptable, 12 months may still be alright, but longer periods could allow competitors too much time to become established. The time delay that is acceptable will vary from project to project – it will always be a factor of importance.

The significance to the customer (i.e. the consumer) of the new development will be of great consequence. If an established leading brand is to be challenged successfully on a performance basis by a new brand then the newcomer will need to have a significant advantage; a marginal advantage is unlikely to be enough. The record book substantiates this, and so it follows that the advantage must be significant if it is to be worth waiting for. On this issue, well constructed product testing with consumers should provide helpful guidance, but sound management judgement will again be vitally important. Giving up the 'first' position could be a high price to pay if the judgement proves to be wrong.

When You Cannot Be 'First'

A particularly interesting strategy decision will always face the big operator who finds that one of his competitors has beaten him to a new market, or existing market development, and he knows that this move is likely to be of real significance in the longer term.

Should the operator accept that he must move into the market as 'second' with a product that is very similar to his competitor who is 'first'? Or should he wait until he has developed a product that will give him a significant advantage over his competitors?

Of course, much will depend on the specific circumstances – in particular, the various strengths and weaknesses of the competitors – but there are a number of key considerations:

1. If he enters the market in a 'second' position he needs to be very confident that he will be able to stop his competitor gaining a dominant leadership. This could be of great importance in the longer term – into the future there could be a major difference between having to displace a dominant leader as against one who is only marginally ahead.

2. Just how sure is the operator that he will be able to produce

the product with a significant competitive advantage? And produce it within a reasonable period of time.

3. The strength and ability of the various competitors in terms of operating efficiency will be of consequence. Sometimes operating efficiency can, in itself, overcome a short-term lead.

4. Financial strength could be of significance. Could the new leader stand up financially to a vigorous counter-attack which includes strong pricing activity?

5. What is the position within the distributive trade? Has the man who is 'first' been able to negotiate exclusive contracts? Has he been able to arrange 'solo' stocking deals with major distributors?

6. Would it make good business sense for the big operator to both enter the market with a 'stopping' brand and then to follow later with a major new brand operation? Much will depend on the importance of the particular market to the operator, and of the various costs and revenues involved, but detailed consideration of such a proposition could be worth while.

■ *To these considerations may be added many others. As is very clear, each position requires particular consideration, there is no one solution. However, it is very obvious that ideally you would wish to avoid the problems that this position brings. The way to do this is to make every effort to ensure that, with all projects that are of importance to you, you are both 'first' and 'right'.*

Be 'First', Be 'Right': *Tide* in the U.S.A. and *Tide* in the U.K.

Through the 1930s the U.S. washing powder market was essentially a soap powder market (i.e. the detergent within the washing powder was based on soap). Research aimed at the development of a suitable synthetic detergent was in progress, but it was limited and had no material influence on the market-place at the time.

The research work continued through the war years. There was an acute shortage of certain of the raw materials which were used to make soap, and so the research was given greater prominence.

By 1946 the Procter and Gamble Company in the U.S. was ready for a test market with a synthetic detergent product. The brand name chosen to carry the development was *Tide*. Patents were arranged in 1946, and at this time the P&G brand was well ahead of its competitors.

Among many observers there was considerable doubt as to how well the 'synthetics' would perform in the market when soap powder raw materials were again freely available. Even in the P&G camp there were some doubters. The company chairman, during the annual meeting in 1947, is reported to have stated "in our judgement, there is small chance of synthetic detergents replacing soap powders to any marked extent. They are marvellous products in some fields, but limited in others and will supplement rather than supplant soap powders in most homes."

In fact, *Tide* was an outstanding success. By 1949 it was in national distribution in the U.S., it quickly became the No. 1 brand, and eventually a dominant market leader. The *Tide* brand has led the U.S. washing powder market for over 40 years, and promises to go on to claim 50, and possibly many more, years of leadership.

With its U.S. *Tide* operation P&G had followed the golden rule very closely. It was certainly 'first'; for the U.S. market the brand was clearly 'right'; and no doubt the company had taken care to have as much 'surprise' as possible in the development of the project.

Tide has become one of the truly great brands in U.S. history. Its dominant leadership position in one of the country's biggest consumer markets has made it a prodigious profit contributor. Many observers would argue that the *Tide* U.S. success has been a 'key' factor in the funding of P&G's subsequent moves into other markets within the U.S. and also into international markets.

In the U.K. in the 1930s, and into the late 1940s, the washing powder market was also essentially a soap powder market. Through this period the clear brand leader of the market was *Persil* (marketed by Crosfields, which was part of the Lever organization).

Procter and Gamble was represented in the U.K. by the Thomas Hedley Co. The business had been purchased by P&G in 1930 and by 1939 had become a considerable force within the U.K. market.

The first synthetic detergent, intended for the main wash, to enter the U.K. market was a Lever brand named *Wisk*. However, *Wisk* encountered technical problems and was never of any real consequence in the market. Actually, with *Wisk*, Lever broke the golden rule – they were 'first', but they were clearly *not* 'right'.

Tide was moved into test market in the U.K. in 1949, and then moved into the Metropolitan London area (covering approximately 25–30% of the U.K. population) in 1950. It completed its national launch in 1952. The brand was the first efficient heavy duty synthetic detergent to enter the U.K. market. It had a lead of some 18 months over competitive brands.

Initially *Tide* performed well in the market-place and for a short period it challenged *Persil* for leadership. However, it soon began to fall back and by the mid-1950s *Persil* was estimated to be outselling *Tide* by approximately 2½ to 1.

Despite a number of re-launches *Tide* continued to lose market share and by the late 1960s/early 1970s it was down to 6–7%. The share level continued to fall and the brand was eventually withdrawn in the 1980s. During this time, soap powder *Persil* had continued as a very strong brand, holding market leadership for most of the period.

Tide was understandably a brand for which the P&G organization had strong feelings. It was not allowed to die easily and received considerable support through most of its life period.

Tide was the 'first' effective synthetic detergent into the U.K. market. It had all the advantages of being first, it was managed by a company with a reputation for highly skilled brand management, and yet it was unsuccessful.

There are a number of views as to why *Tide* experienced difficulty in the U.K. It would seem to be generally agreed that its initial formula was a major problem.

Persil, the U.K. market leader, contained a relatively high level of an ingredient named sodium perborate, which is a very effective bleaching agent in boiling/hot water, and in the 1950s and 60s a high proportion of the wash in the U.K. was carried out in boiling/hot water. In the U.S. it was customary for women to add a liquid bleach to their wash: in the U.K. the position was different, and there was a wide expectation that the washing powder should contain a bleach. The earlier versions of *Tide* in the U.K. (as with the U.S. product) did not contain perborate (if it was used, it was at a relatively low level).

Daz, a brand launched by P&G in the U.K. in 1953, was formulated similarly to *Tide* but with sodium perborate, and it went on to achieve a much higher level of success than *Tide.*

With *Tide* in the U.K., P&G broke the golden rule. *Tide* was certainly 'first', but it was *not* 'right' for the U.K. market, and so it experienced difficulties.

Surprise

It is very important to be first. It is equally important to be right. And if you also have 'surprise' on your side then your position should indeed be strong.

Army generals – who talk and write frequently on the great significance of having a winning strategy – have no doubt as to the outstanding value of surprise. Carl von Clausewitz, the Prussian soldier so much respected and so often quoted from his writings on military strategy, has no doubt whatsoever as to the value of surprise. In his book *On War* (*Von Kriege*), published in 1832, he writes "The surprise is, therefore, not only the means to the attainment of numerical superiority; but it is also to be regarded as a substantive principle in itself, on account of its moral effect. When it is successful in a high degree, confusion and broken courage in the enemy's ranks are the consequences; and of the degree to which these multiply a success, there are examples enough, great and small."

There is no doubt that many modern day generals, including those who have operated successfully in recent wars, would agree wholeheartedly with Clausewitz.

Many of the golden rules of business strategy and operations have their beginnings in military studies and experiences. 'Surprise' is certainly no exception to this.

Business is a form of war. For real success in business it is necessary to out-think and out-manoeuvre your competitors (the enemy); when appropriate, to move faster than they do; and to get yourself into a position to dictate the cause and outcome of the action. A successful general is involved in a similar manner in a military action. This is why successful business and military men so frequently agree on the golden rules of strategy and operations.

In a war the great advantage of surprise is very obvious. If you can catch your enemy when he is unprepared you can use your forces to advance through his territory, occupy his towns and cities, control his vital command centres, and so on. And you can do this with the use of a limited number and expenditure of your own forces. Most importantly, it can all be achieved before your enemy is fully aware of what is happening.

The history of war has many examples which illustrate the advantage and value of surprise. So also has the history of business. If the enemy (the competitors) can be caught by surprise by, for instance, a new brand launch, then the initial attack can be made before he has been able to erect any form of defence. The vitally important initial sampling should be possible and a follow-up 'consolidation' promotion (part of the pursuit) could also be mounted before any worthwhile opposition is organized.

The same basic considerations apply for other business moves, such as the launch of a new form of packaging, a new promotional idea, a new delivery system, and so forth. All such operations can benefit considerably if they have 'surprise'.

■ *Again the message is both clear and simple – You should take all reasonable action to ensure you have surprise on your side with both your strategic and operational activities.*

The qualification of 'reasonable' action is made merely to cover the point that while surprise is invariably of great value, as we shall see as we discuss it further, it can have a cost which may need to be limited.

Surprise does not Guarantee Success

It should be clear that while surprise can be a great asset it does not necessarily guarantee success. If the particular business proposition is basically unsound then it will fail even if it is supported by complete surprise.

Surprise should always help. A proposition that has minor weaknesses could break through and achieve a reasonable success with the aid of surprise; without surprise it would probably fail. This is one of the key factors about surprise. While it certainly cannot guarantee success, lack of it can often greatly increase the probability of failure.

The issue is really concerned with a forecast of what your competitors are able to do with or without notice of your activity. If your competitors are all sleepy and very inactive companies then advance notice of your activities may not affect them unduly. In this instance surprise will have a relatively low value.

If your competitors are well-managed, active companies then advance notice of the activities may mean that they take immediate action to thwart your operations. In this case surprise will have a very high relative value.

Degrees of Surprise

The aim should be absolute security which brings complete surprise. When the new brand, new development, or whatever innovation is the subject of the operation, actually moves into the market, this should be the first indication that competitors have of its existence.

Complete surprise should be the aim but often it will be difficult, probably impossible, to obtain this. Some form of leak is likely to occur. It may be the result of carelessness, of an accident, or just very good intelligence work by competitors – absolute secrecy is likely to be broken. This applies for almost any large-scale project where many people both inside and outside of the company are involved.

There is, of course, a great difference between a total lack of security and a small leak. If we agree that total security is very difficult to achieve, then the aim must be to ensure that if there are any leaks they should be small ones and of very limited significance within the total operation.

What this means is that in any operation all factors are of importance, but some are crucial. If a competitor gets to know that a new brand is likely to appear late in the year, this could be damaging; if he gets to know the exact extent and date of the launch, this could be much more than just damaging, it could actually mean a failure for the operation.

With every operation there will be a limited number of 'key' factors – these are of vital importance to the success of the operation. On these factors the highest level of security should be maintained.

How to Surprise your Competitors

Any business that wants success must be sure it has surprise on its side. How does it set about ensuring that its operations, their timing and their content, come as a surprise, preferably a complete surprise, to its competitors? The straightforward answer is that it must 'batten down the hatches' and keep them battened down.

Breaks in security destroy the element of surprise, so they must be avoided. The breaks come from people – the people of the business and others who are closely associated with it. If the break does not come from people talking, then it comes from their actions.

■ *There are two basic steps that a company wishing to have 'surprise' on its side should take:*

First, limit the number of people who have access to 'key' information; the smaller the number of people with access, the better.

Second, ensure that those who have access to 'key' information are fully aware of their responsibility to keep security, and meet this responsibility. To break security must be seen, and treated, as a most serious offence.

Leaks normally occur through either carelessness or an accident. The more people who have access to 'key' information, the greater is the possibility of a leak.

■ *In deciding who should have access to a particular piece of information it is worth asking the question "Does this person need this specific information to carry out his responsibilities effectively?" This is a very different question to the one that asks "Would this person find this information interesting?"*

If, within the business, access to information is limited to those who really need it as against those who would like to have it, then the possibility of a leak will be greatly reduced (so also will the amount of paper circulating in the business, and the amount of time taken up in 'interesting' discussion).

There is clearly a need for everyone in the business, and particularly those who have access to the 'key' information, to be very security minded, and to be sure that they personally are not the cause of a security break.

The requirement goes beyond the direct employees of the company and also includes other personnel (e.g. the staff of an advertising agency) who have access to the 'key' information.

There will be a need for a strong lead from the top of the business which makes clear how highly security is rated. And the words will need to be backed by appropriate action wherever necessary.Similarly, all suppliers and advisers should be informed of the company's attitude toward security and they will be expected to apply the highest standards to their personnel.

■ *The obvious occasions for leaks are usually recognized and avoided by all personnel. It is on the exceptional occasion that the slip frequently occurs. The chemist who is addressing a professional society lets slip the results of a recent experiment; a salesman talks of the success of a recent consumer test; or an advertising man talks with a friend of his new creative challenge; and so forth. These are typical examples of 'careless leaks' which can cause problems and prove very expensive.*

In Search of 'Leaks'

'Leaks' are of great importance. Every company should take security action to ensure that its plans remain confidential. It follows that equally every company should be taking legitimate action to find out the development plans and proposed actions of its competitors. To know in advance just what your competitor is planning to do in a particular market could be invaluable. You can take action to counter his proposals, and prepare for your own attack. Better still you could arrange to take action in advance of his. Clearly any competitor should be searching for 'leaks'.

We are talking here of taking legitimate action to find out what your competitors plan to do. That is, action within the law. For instance, a company could have an expenditure budget specifically aimed at taking lawful action to view competitive production facilities, attend conferences where competitive staff are speaking, survey stores thought to be carrying new competitive product on test, and so forth.

All members of staff should be required to make a special effort to get to know of any new development activities undertaken by competitors. Salesmen, researchers, advertising personnel, buyers, all members of staff can encounter legitimate opportunities to get to know of competitive activities. If all the incoming information, from all the various sources, is recorded in a systematic manner, then it could begin to provide an outline of a competitive move, and if this is followed up, it could prove extremely valuable.

Is Subterfuge Worth While?

Before attempting to answer this question it is necessary to explain the meaning attributed to the word subterfuge here. The term subterfuge here is intended to cover the use of deliberate deception on a substantial scale.

The general who, before he makes his major attack on the main central front, arranges for his patrols to enter into skirmishes in both the north and the south has employed a form of subterfuge. He is attempting to divert attention so that his main attack will have a greater element of surprise.

In the definition of subterfuge above, the qualification 'on a substantial scale' has been added to the normally accepted definition. This is merely to give the question more substance: to ask if it is worth making a serious effort to deceive your competitors – and a serious effort would involve deliberate investment in terms of personnel, time, money, and other resources. The answer to the question is very simply "Yes, it is worth engaging in subterfuge providing it can be shown to work, and also providing it does not detract unduly from the main effort of the enterprise."

As with all business investments, a question that should also be asked is "Will it bring at least a satisfactory level of return?" Of course, for the form of investment we are considering here, measuring the return with any worthwhile degree of confidence will be impossible. The investment will be, to some considerable extent, a judgement investment.

■ *Really successful subterfuge will do more than help obtain 'surprise', it will also cause the enemy (competitors) to waste effort and resources.*

If the general's skirmishes in the south and the north caused his enemy to redirect his defensive forces to these areas then they will have achieved much more than just helping to ensure surprise. The enemy will have been involved in a series of wasteful, frustrating, and time consuming manoeuvres.

Similarly if a manufacturer manages to convince his competitors that his new brand is intended to attack the high-quality/high-price sector of a given market, while in fact he intends to invade the lower price/high-volume sector, then he may well cause his competitors to waste considerable effort. Their attempts to develop a high-quality brand or to adjust their existing brands could well be a waste of effort, and have taken up resources that could have been used on the main market defence.

There will be a need to keep a strict control on the extent of any investment in subterfuge. Frequently the activities concerned are not of a high-level investment nature. Perfectly genuine public statements of the options the company is considering can often be effective subterfuge.

Many companies do not engage consciously in any form of subterfuge. They put their full effort into ensuring that their security systems and approach are maintained in the best possible order. They reason that subterfuge is unnecessary and could possibly cause confusion for their own personnel.

It is necessary to explain that the remarks under this heading refer to legitimate subterfuge. There is sometimes a feeling that subterfuge moves are illegal and unethical. If they are illegal they clearly should not be practised. If a manufacturer considers a proposed move possibly unethical then he must decide for himself whether or not to follow it.

But subterfuge in general is neither illegal nor unethical. If a manufacturer is asked where he is putting his major development effort and he feels he should reply, it is surely reasonable that he quote the ten areas he covers. The fact that in nine of the areas he has only minor activity and in one a very major effort is not a consideration he needs to make public. Many acts of subterfuge take this form.

The Cost of Surprise

There is a cost involved in maintaining a high level of security and in this way ensuring that you have 'surprise' on your side.

It is a difficult cost to calculate with any confidence of accuracy. Some of it will be in the form of material items, but most of it will be in management time bringing a 'security conscious' approach to everyone in the business. Beyond this there is the task of ensuring that others – who are outside the business, but are in possession of confidential information – are also 'security conscious'. It will be vitally important that the senior management follows the practice of 'leadership by example' on this particular subject. If they are lax in their security the whole company will be lax; if they are controlled and responsible the company will follow their lead. To be responsible in this respect is *not* a costly business.

■ *If we consider the outstanding benefits a company is likely to obtain if it is able to keep all its operations a 'complete surprise' from its competitors then the relatively small expenditure involved in maintaining the highest possible level of security must be one of the best yielding investments the business is likely to make.*

When 'Surprise' is not Required

We have talked so strongly of the great value of 'surprise' that it seems almost unbelievable that there can be occasions when a manufacturer may decide that he does not want 'surprise' on his side. These occasions are rare and they tend to be of a very special nature. It should also be clear that the decision to forego 'surprise' should be accepted only after very careful consideration.

Among such special occasions, the following are likely to be the most prominent:

1. *Where it is known that satisfactory security is impossible.*
   For instance, it could be that certain statutory regulations require that manufacturers have to disclose their product formula to a public body responsible for testing before it can enter the market.
   Where special (e.g. safety) arrangements are necessary before distribution can be undertaken.
   For instance, special storage and transport arrangements may be necessary.
   When exceptional conditions of this kind apply the manufacturer may decide that his best move is to dispense with any attempt at full security and to make public certain of his moves well in advance. There could be occasions when the advance publicity could be made to work favourably.

2. *In an attempt to 'frighten off' competitors.*
   If you are the 'big' man in a market where all the other competitors are 'small' operators you may believe that by making your plans public you will give warning that you will 'stand no nonsense' from the small fellows. To do this you need to be very sure of your competitive position. You are in fact saying to your competitors "I intend this particular market position to be mine, and you will get badly hurt if you challenge me". The big man who uses this approach will need to act ruthlessly if any of the small men should challenge him. He will need to build a reputation as a man who 'always defends his established position without regard to short-term cost'. Of course, the plans that are published must outline a very strong attacking position, one that within the particular market would be recognized as almost unassailable.
   While this approach would normally be concerned with the

publication of marketing plans it can also apply for production capacity.

If the man in possession of the market makes it known that he is investing in additional capacity to take care of any market expansion, then competitors will have been given notice that he will fight desperately to ensure that his new plant does not stand idle.

3. *Where there is a clear advantage to be gained from early disclosure.*

If the early disclosure will bring a commitment to purchase from a number of vitally important customers, then early disclosure may be very worth while. This can frequently apply with items of large and complex capital goods. Without the commitment of certain of the very limited number of customers in the market, production may be uneconomic and a great risk. It can also mean that in certain circumstances 'key' distributors can be persuaded to agree to sign exclusive contracts (i.e. the distributor would not distribute competitive brands).

■ *The message of this golden rule is both simple and straightforward, and is worthy of repetition:*
"Be sure your business has a successful strategy backed by effective and efficient operations; then encourage your people to use their skill and enthusiasm to ensure you are 'first' and 'right'. In the process take the necessary action to have 'surprise' on your side. The management that can achieve this must surely move forward to considerable business success."

Chapter 4

Real Business Success Demands a Competitive Advantage

*Define it, develop it, exploit it,
and be sure to protect it.*

In all markets there are winners and losers. The winners always have some form of competitive advantage over the losers and they are able to use this to achieve superior results.

Successful businesses search for opportunities. They assess and evaluate the opportunities they find, and then select for operation those they believe they can develop and exploit more effectively than their competitors. They select for operation those opportunities where they believe they can develop a significant competitive advantage.

The competitive advantage is vitally important, its development and exploitation is at the centre of every brand or product success. Without a competitive advantage there is unlikely to be any real success.

■ *The message of this golden rule is clear. Successful brands make a successful company, and a successful brand invariably has a significant competitive advantage. If you want success you must be sure to build within your business an ability, and a practice, to develop and exploit competitive advantage.*

What is a Competitive Advantage?

A competitive advantage is quite simply an advantage your competitors do not have. It can be, for instance, a special formula development, a product manufacturing-cost advantage, a particular skill in operating, or the establishment of an exclusive channel of product distribution. The important point is that it is an advantage which is restricted to the operator concerned – his competitors do not have it.

All competitive advantages eventually find their way through to the brand or product best value equation. This is why the competitive advantage is of such major importance – the more significant it is to the customer, the more important it is to the manufacturer.

Either directly or indirectly, a competitive advantage enables its owner to give his customers an 'extra', an added value, something his competitors cannot offer. It can be in terms of brand purpose, performance, price, or presentation, or a combination of these factors.

To be classed as a competitive advantage within the scope of this golden rule an advantage must have the ability to at least recover its cost. The recovery can be in terms of selling the same volume at a higher unit price, or by increasing total revenue and contribution by selling a higher total volume. If it is unable to do this it may possibly remain an advantage but it would not be worthy of the title 'competitive advantage'. Recovery of the cost is, of course, a minimum position: a worthwhile competitive advantage would expect to achieve much more than mere cost recovery.

■ *All competitive advantages are worth having, but those that are big enough to make an impact on the market-place and on the competitive positions within it are the ones the operator should concentrate the skill and effort of the business to produce. Competitive advantages with this wider and more substantial ability are known as 'significant'.*

Competitive Advantage and Business Success

All successful brands (i.e. brands which are able to hold leadership of their particular market sectors and return a satisfactory level of profit) have a significant competitive advantage.

If the competitive advantage is a superior performance then it is probable that the brand can obtain a higher price, or a better volume. With skilful management both a higher price and a better volume could be possible.

If the competitive advantage provides a lower unit cost then there will be an opportunity to use price more competitively to gain volume, or to take a higher unit contributory margin which in turn can be used to improve brand volume or profit.

Where the business has foreseen the development of a new consumer need ahead of its competitors and has been able to produce a brand to meet this need, this should provide it with a competitive advantage. Searching out, developing, and exploiting the opportunity ahead of all others should mean that it (i.e. the particular benefit provided) is linked directly to the brand.

The success of a business is measured in terms of its performance in creating and satisfying customers, and in meeting its profit objectives. Competitive advantages will be essential for a satisfactory level of business performance.

In business strategy there will be a need to identify the opportunity and then to decide the competitive advantage needed to exploit it to the full. There is the further requirement that the necessary resources should be concentrated on the development of the competitive advantages and that it should be available in a practicable form ahead of the competition.

The strategy may specify its requirements very clearly, but operations have to make it happen. In many respects the approach to operations will be similar to that for strategy. The time period covered may be much shorter, the need for action more urgent; nevertheless the basic approach should be the same.

The operator will have available to him a number of ways in which he can manage a particular shorter term position. Each way is, in effect, an opportunity. The important requirement is to select for action that opportunity which will be most effective in meeting the shorter term objective. The operator's ability to mount an action with which he has a competitive advantage should clearly be a key factor in his decision as to which opportunity he selects for operation.

■ *In the consideration of both the strategic and operations proposals the 'key' requirement, following the identification of the opportunity, is the recognition of the competitive advantage necessary to develop and exploit it, and an assessment of the ability of the company, and of its competitors, to produce the advantage and in what time period.*

Without a significant competitive advantage an attack on a leading brand is unlikely to succeed; without at least a competitive advantage an attack on either the second or third brand in the market is unlikely to have any success.

Sometimes an operator may be wise to let what appears to be the most desirable opportunity in a market pass if he feels sure that others are much better equipped to develop and exploit the competitive advantage necessary to meet it. Better that he concentrate his efforts on a slightly less desirable opportunity but one where he has a real lead in the development of the competitive advantage, and where he can expect to be first with a fully competent exploitation.

■ *Markets where rivals 'slug it out' with brands or products which are almost identical in every respect (i.e. neither brand has a competitive advantage) are unlikely to provide adequate profit levels to the contestants. Such markets invariably drift into becoming price markets, where the only brand differential which applies is that of the periodic 'lower price special'.*

Business success and competitive advantage go together. Business managers should be fully aware of this fact and should take active steps to ensure that everyone in the business is aware of the need for, and value of, competitive advantage.

Development of Competitive Advantage

Significant competitive advantages are clearly of great value to an operating business. How are they developed?

A competitive advantage can arise by chance. By accident, a chemist mixes two ingredients and finds they deliver a better result than did the prescribed formula. The new product is exceptionally good, good enough to represent a competitive advantage in performance. If a company is especially lucky it may develop a competitive advantage this way, say, once every ten years. But it will need to be exceptionally lucky.

A company that is serious about making real progress will not be prepared to rely on being exceptionally lucky – it will take positive action.

The development of a competitive advantage is very much the concern of the people of a business. They will need the necessary skill, and they will have to contribute a satisfactory level of effort. But most important of all they will need to bring the 'right' attitude to the task. This is a field where a sagacious approach, backed by a strong, sensible enthusiasm, and well-designed motivation, will be necessary to achieve a leadership position.

There will need to be an acceptance of the approach which says 'There is always a better way', and a drive to ensure that the company finds it and puts it into operation before competitors do.

It is suggested that when a business has people with the necessary skills, who are prepared to make an appropriate effort, and have the 'right' attitude, a 'sensible' systematic approach is likely to bring the best results.

A 'sensible' systematic approach is one that combines the appropriate disciplines with a degree of freedom which encourages the individuals concerned to use their initiatives and, on occasions, to follow their hunches. Achieving the right balance in this approach can be difficult but for satisfactory results in this form of activity it is very necessary.

A systematic approach is likely to concentrate on two areas:

1. To meet a marketing opportunity;
2. As a planned activity in the business via
    (a) functional (or departmental) activity and
    (b) company projects.

1. MARKETING OPPORTUNITIES

The business should be engaged in a continuous search for marketing opportunities. All those markets in which the business competes in earnest, and which are considered to have potential, should be the subject of a series of research studies. These studies should consider the consumers' views of the brands currently in the market, their strengths and their weaknesses. In particular the studies should cover the consumer needs and requirements not currently serviced by the brands already available. The new markets which the business is considering for entry should also be the subject of similar research.

■ *The most valuable competitive advantages, those that can make a significant difference to a brand's competitive position in the market-place, are invariably associated with the 'key' brand attributes contained within the best value concept. They are usually associated with brand purpose, performance, price, or presentation. Frequently they will be associated with more than one of the attributes. This is very understandable as these attributes bear directly on the brand's value to the consumer.*

The first manufacturer to discover a new purpose should be well positioned to develop and exploit it in the market-place ahead of his competitors. If he does this effectively he can make the particular purpose the property of his brand.

Competitive Advantage – Purpose

Product competitive advantages are normally associated with skilled, and often extensive, research investment. However, sometimes they can come from relatively simple developments.

The U.K. lavatory cleaner market in 1980 was led by two powder brands – *Harpic* (Reckitt and Colman) and *Dot* (Lever). The market was estimated to be worth approximately £5m.

Lever was considering a new entry to the market and was looking for a competitive advantage to build into its proposed new brand. The new brand was to be in liquid form.

From consumer research it appeared that there were two main consumer requirements – an ability to kill germs, and to clean the lavatory.

Lever chemists were able to produce a product that met both of these requirements satisfactorily; however, they were not able to provide a worthwhile competitive advantage in the performance.

Further research revealed that the consumer had another priority requirement and this was that after the use of the product the lavatory should have a fresh smell.

An examination of the brands in the market showed that none of them met this threefold requirement – to kill germs, clean, and smell fresh.

The Lever chemists were given the task of meeting the treble requirement, and they produced a product that scored very well on each one of the required attributes in consumer tests.

The product became part of the brand *Frish*. At the time it was the only brand in the market to meet the consumers' three main requirements. This gave the brand a competitive advantage and it was launched into the U.K. national market in 1982. It was an outstanding success. The total market doubled to some £10m, and *Frish* claimed a brand share of over 50%.

Lever was unable to give the *Frish* competitive advantage any high degree of protection. Other brands quickly followed its lead and attempted to provide a fresh smell.

The Lever marketing approach for *Frish* moved quickly to ensure that the successful introduction was followed by a strong 'pursuit'. Despite the many 'copy' brands *Frish* was able to consolidate its position and remained a strong market leader.

The *Frish* competitive advantage had come primarily from skilled consumer research. The Lever researchers had discovered a consumer requirement (purpose) that was not fulfilled by the brands in the market. Although it was an advantage that could be copied rapidly it was enough to allow a skilled marketing team to form a new brand and move it to market leadership.

The advantage of superiority in performance is clear. Of course, it is important that the particular performance advance should be of consequence to the consumer and available at a reasonable price.

Competitive Advantage – Performance

Lever Bros., through its parent company Unilever, purchased the Domestos business in 1961. The main brand marketed by the company was *Domestos,* the leader of the U.K. household bleach market.

Domestos had originally been marketed on a promise to remove certain difficult stains in clothes washing. However, with the incorporation of bleach in many washing powders the company had decided to change the promise to 'kills all known germs'. This was a successful change for the brand; the 'bleach included' washing powders had made its position as an ancillary to the washing powder market a very limited one, and the 'kills all known germs' promise gave it a very strong position in terms of household hygiene.

Lever was very keen to develop the *Domestos* brand and it benefited from the additional research and marketing investment put behind it. *Domestos* was a very strong bleach, and this was its main advantage over its competitors. The brand was sold at a price which represented a substantial premium over its weaker rivals.

The *Domestos* product looked almost the same as its weaker and cheaper competitors, and the consumer was unable to see its 'germ killing' ability in action. Given this position Lever had some difficulty in giving *Domestos* a full exploitation.

In the late 1960s the Lever research and development unit found a means of thickening the *Domestos* product. This provided the brand with a most valuable competitive advantage.

Firstly, the thickening allowed the *Domestos* product to cling to lavatory walls and similar surfaces for much longer than its thinner competitors, and so it was able to perform more effectively.

Secondly, the thickening differentiated the *Domestos* brand and its customers were able to see that it was different. At this time *Domestos* was the only thick bleach available.

Thirdly, and very importantly, the thickening enabled the *Domestos* brand to demonstrate its superiority over other bleaches in a competitive manner in advertising. Now the brand and its advantages could be exploited fully.

The thickening of *Domestos* represented a significant competitive advantage. The *Domestos* brand went on to consolidate its market leadership right through the 1970s and beyond. It became one of the most successful brands in the U.K. grocery markets.

Price is always an important area for gaining a competitive advantage, and a more competitive price has very obvious attractions for consumers.

Competitive Advantage – Price

Price can be used aggressively by an operator whether or not he has a unit cost advantage. However, only if he has a unit cost advantage, for an equivalent product, can a price move rate as one based on a competitive advantage.

It is possible to gain a cost advantage if you have a very high volume and a reasonable level of efficiency. It is also possible to have a cost advantage if you have very high efficiency and a reasonable level of volume.

Any operator who wants to use price aggressively needs to be very sure he has a competitive advantage, preferably a significant one, in unit cost. For this he needs a volume level which places him well ahead of his competitors, with an operating efficiency which is also at the highest level. Only if he has this double achievement can he be fully confident he is 'the lowest cost producer' and well equipped for price action.

From the second half of the 1970s and on into the 1980s *Persil Automatic* was the outstanding leader of the U.K. washing powder market. For much of the time the brand outsold its nearest rival by 2 to 1.

Persil Automatic was manufactured at Lever's Warrington plant in the North West of England. The plant specialized in the production of a very limited number of Lever brands of which *Persil Automatic* was the most prominent.

Lever had good reason to believe that its Warrington plant achieved a very high level of operating efficiency, possibly the highest level in Europe for this form of plant.

The company was also very confident that its buyers were fully effective, and that its sales force was highly competent in its negotiations with the U.K. grocery trade.

Given this position Lever had every confidence that, with *Persil Automatic,* in terms of unit cost, it held a very worthwhile competitive advantage over its rivals. The company had the choice of either taking this advantage into additional brand margin or of using it in competitive pricing.

Throughout this period Lever chose to follow a low unit margin policy with *Persil Automatic,* and this was clearly a very important factor in the brand's highly successful development.

[See the Low Unit Margin case study in Chapter 8]

An outstanding brand presentation can work wonders for brand trial. And if a brand is to become the best value choice of a consumer it is essential that he should try it.

Competitive Advantage – Presentation

Within brand presentation, advertising is invariably an important consideration. Advertising has three tasks: (1) to persuade consumers to try the brand, (2) to provide existing users of the brand with assurance, confidence, and encouragement to continue buying, and (3) to play its part in developing the desired brand personality.

It is important to note that while these advertising tasks are always present, they are not necessarily present at the same level of intensity for each one at any given time.

Probably the most important criteria for an effective brand advertisement are that it should do an outstanding job in bringing about brand trial, and re-trial, and that it should do this in a manner, tone, and setting which ensures that it plays a full part in forming the desired brand personality. If an advertisement does this effectively, it has the prospect of developing a competitive advantage for its brand.

The U.K. soaps, detergent and household cleaner markets have seen a number of outstanding brand presentations which have helped to build competitive advantages.

It is widely agreed that the skilful presentation of *Persil*, and later *Persil Automatic*, has given the brands very favourable personalities which have enhanced their value. In particular, the *Persil* and *Persil*

Automatic advertising, always in a style and tone that is caring and friendly, always well produced, always simple in approach, and always consistent in its message, has been able to command a conspicuous position within the field of washing powder advertising.

Fairy Liquid has been the most successful U.K. dishwashing liquid. Its brand strength has centred on its high level performance and its mildness. Over the years its presentation has always followed a distinctive style – a style and a tone which have emphasized the mildness benefit.

Ariel was the first enzymatic washing powder in national distribution in the U.K. Enzymes are chemical ingredients which are very effective in removing certain stains from fabrics, and they work particularly well when used in a soak. The television advertising which introduced *Ariel* to many consumers in 1968–70 featured a comparison of the performance of *Ariel* and a non-enzymatic powder in stain removal in a soak situation. This outstanding performance demonstration definitely acted to enhance the aura of efficiency which was an important part of the *Ariel* brand personality.

The main benefit supplied by *Comfort*, the U.K.'s leading fabric softener, is softness. The earlier *Comfort* brand advertisements have always featured this, and softness was conveyed not only in the message but also in the style of presentation. This skilful presentation certainly helped *Comfort* to obtain the dominant leadership of its market.

When a marketing opportunity has been highlighted it should be evaluated and assessed. Part of this procedure will be a consideration as to how well positioned the business is to develop a significant competitive advantage to provide for the exploitation of the opportunity.

Following the selection of the opportunity for action, appropriate resources should be concentrated on the development of the required competitive advantage.

It is always possible for the competitive advantage to come first and for the marketing opportunity to follow. For instance, a technologist finds that a new production process provides certain special qualities not available from other brands. Consumer research shows that these qualities are welcomed and valued by the consumer. Here the competitive advantage has given rise to a new marketing opportunity.

The brand development programme should always be looking ahead and should have a number of the marketing opportunities it has discovered lined up for exploitation into the future, possibly covering the next five years. Some of these will be major opportunities, others will be of a minor nature. In each case the aim should be the development of a competitive advantage to aid the exploitation.

Competitive advantages developed to meet a marketing opportunity would normally be sponsored and piloted through the organization by the marketing department. Part of the responsibility of the brand manager should be to ensure that he is fully aware of the opportunities that may be available to his brand with consumers in the market. Beyond this he should maintain a constant liaison with other sections of the business to ensure that the competitive advantages necessary to exploit the selected opportunities are progressed and brought forward for operation.

2. PLANNED ACTIVITIES

The development of competitive advantages through planned activity in the business should concern every department, every section, and every person, within the business.

(a) Functional departments and sections

Within each functional department and section there should be a planned and active approach to achieve a continuous improvement in performance: the production departments can improve their productivity levels: the sales department can work at its sales approach, use its people more effectively and advance its overall performance; the administrative section can find a means of producing its invoices and delivery notes more efficiently; and so on. If these developments take the business ahead of its competitors they are, in fact, competitive advantages.

Sometimes they may be big enough in themselves to rate as significant; more frequently they are likely to be minor advantages but nevertheless certainly worth having. These minor advantages, coming from a whole series of departments, could well represent in total a significant competitive advantage.

■ *Developments under this heading should have a particular value to the chief executive. They provide him with a means of motivating his departmental heads who in turn can lead their staff forward to higher levels of sectional and personal performance. They provide a means of getting everyone in the business actively concerned in the pursuit of competitive advantage.*

(b) Company projects

Frequently it will be necessary for two or more departments to join together in a particular operation if the optimum gain to the business is to be realized. For instance, joint action between the sales and distribution departments in setting price list order levels, and thereby influencing distribution vehicle loadings, could bring about savings in distribution costs. The term 'company project' is used to describe joint operations of this type.

There should be great scope for activities of this kind in every company. Every part of the business should be the subject of a periodic review. There is always a better way, and this applies to every section.

Projects of this kind provide a means of bringing together personnel with varying skills and experiences, and allowing them time to analyse and review, for instance, a section of the business, a brand, or a particular company procedure, with the aim of improving performance.

■ *Used skilfully company projects can also have a motivating value to the chief executive. They provide a means of bringing the younger, very bright, people into a direct working relationship with more experienced senior personnel. When a project team with this make-up is led wisely the results can often be outstanding.*

The advantage coming from a project team exercise can, on occasions, be of significance but it is more likely to be at a lower level. However, when the results of a number of project teams are totalled, then a significant advantage could well be possible.

Exploitation

A business may have used skill and ingenuity to develop a competitive advantage, but it is of very limited value until it is actually working in the market-place

The type, form and extent of the exploitation of a competitive advantage must depend very much on its evaluation. If it is seen as significant by the customer, and is a factor of consequence in terms of the brand's 'best value' position, then it should be considered for extensive exploitation. Just what this represents will depend very much on the particular market, on the competitive position within it, and on the position of the business concerned.

The basic point is that a competitive advantage is unlikely to influence a potential customer unless he knows about it, and is able to appreciate the benefit it provides. Given that the advantage is in performance, the requirement is that he has the opportunity to try the brand/product. Only in use can any performance benefit really be fully appreciated.

If the advantage is in the form of a price differential then the potential customer needs to be aware of this and to see it in competition with the prices of other brands. This means that the brand/product needs to have store distribution and price display. Or the price position needs to be conveyed to the customer in some other form.

Should the competitive advantage be a new purpose, some means of communicating this to the potential customer will be essential if it is to influence the buying decision.

If the competitive advantage is in the form of a new and enlightened presentation, then clearly for this to influence the customer it is essential that it be seen and/or heard.

■ *From all of this it must be clear that for a competitive advantage to contribute to its full potential a skilled and comprehensive exploitation will be essential. Indeed, if a competitive advantage lends itself to extensive and effective exploitation then its value is markedly increased.*

When a performance competitive advantage can be demonstrated, and in particular when the superiority can be demonstrated competitively (i.e. in comparison with a competing brand), then the marketing man has a very effective exploitation 'tool' to support his brand.

Just what kind of exploitation should be employed will depend on the particular circumstances. But if it is not carried out effectively and in a suitably rapid time period then the value of the competitive advantage could be lost. Competitors will be studying developments closely and if they are able to copy the improvement and put their own brand development into the market with a suitable exploitation they could make the major advance.

It is important to appreciate that the operator will probably have only one opportunity to get his advantage home to the customer. Normally, a new brand is made or broken in its first year. It may be re-launched in its second or third year but if it has failed at its launch it is unlikely to be fully successful.

The same remarks can be applied to the exploitation of a competitive advantage. If it fails in its initial introduction then it is unlikely to enjoy real success later. Hence, the requirement is that the exploitation should be carried out effectively and every effort made to ensure that it is comprehensive enough in its approach to make full use of the potential of the particular competitive advantage.

"You should do your main work on the exploitation of a competitive advantage before you start on its development." In that the identification of, for instance, a very worthwhile marketing opportunity should have provided the base for the eventual exploitation, this statement is basically correct. Although, of course, the actual task of exploitation will still need to be carried out effectively and efficiently.

■ *The important requirement is that detailed consideration should be given to the exploitation well before the particular competitive advantage is ready for the market-place.*

A marketing opportunity (i.e. a consumer need or benefit not adequately serviced by existing brands already in the market) may have been correctly identified. Just how to present this benefit to the potential customer is a consideration that could require extensive research and experimentation. And if the presentation is along the wrong lines the opportunity may be missed. Even worse, the opportunity may be presented to a competitor.

What at first appears to be a minor competitive advantage can often be changed into one of real consequence. Finding exactly the right promise and then featuring it in a first class presentation can often turn what promises to be a moderate success into something which is outstanding. But of course if the operator is relying on highly skilled presentation *alone* to provide the significant advantage he is certainly taking a major risk.

Competitive Advantage and Brand Marketing Success

In very simple terms, an outline for a brand marketing success would read:

- Find the marketing opportunity. Assess and evaluate it.
- Define the *competitive advantage* necessary to exploit the opportunity.
- Decide whether or not you are positioned to develop and exploit the *competitive advantage* more effectively, and more rapidly, than your competitors.
- Accept (or reject) the marketing opportunity for action.
- If you accept, concentrate resources on the development of the opportunity and in particular of the *competitive advantage*.
- Marketing opportunities are exploited by brands. The *competitive advantage* must be incorporated into a brand, either an established brand or a new one.
- When you have developed the *competitive advantage* check its value with the ultimate customer. If you have a *competitive advantage* of real significance be sure you exploit it to the full.
- Be sure the key factor within the brand *competitive advantage* is given all available protection.

The cost of exploitation is always a factor which should be considered well in advance of any move into the market.

With the smaller advantages extensive calculations and planning are unlikely to be justified. If, for instance, the advantage brings a relatively small decrease in production costs then this may be allowed to increase the gross margin produced by the brand/s concerned and to be used generally rather than in a specific manner. However, with the big significant competitive advantages it is vitally important that plans should be made which provide for production and marketing.

It may well be advisable for a manufacturer to forego what appears to be the most attractive marketing opportunity available simply because he cannot finance its exploitation.

Evaluation

To over-value a competitive advantage can prove to be an expensive mistake. For instance, the new formula which is rated so very highly by the chemists in research and is therefore given the full treatment in the market-place, may not rate so highly with customers. And the new form of packaging which at first appeared so novel and attractive can quickly lose its appeal.

Everyone who has spent a lengthy period in practical business operations will have experience of competitive advantages which have failed to live up to their early promise. The cost they incur centres on the time and resources which are placed behind them but then fail to provide an adequate return.

It is always possible that the greatest cost will be incurred when a significant competitive advantage is under-valued. With an under-valuation the opportunity cost could be particularly high, and this is especially so where a competitor has appreciated what has happened and has moved in with his own development.

All of this points to a need to get the evaluation of your competitive advantage 'right'. How can you be sure to do this? As with all matters of this kind you can never be sure, but you should be able to avoid the major pitfalls.

The competitive advantages that are concerned with an ability to produce at a lower cost level can usually be measured with a reasonable degree of accuracy and should not be difficult to evaluate. Competitive advantages which are difficult to evaluate are those where a high degree of judgement is involved. Marketing research in its various forms should be helpful. It should certainly be able to distinguish between the very good and the very bad. But the real problem will be deciding between 'the good', the 'very good', and the 'outstanding'. And the difference is of great consequence.

The 'outstanding' will clearly be a significant competitive advantage. With this it may be worth attempting a market break for clear leadership, even against an established leader. But the risk could be high; the established leader is likely to fight hard and be prepared to fight for a long time. A correct evaluation of your competitive advantage will be essential.

Significant competitive advantages are difficult to come by. They should not be wasted. They require careful and detailed evaluation. They require good judgement. But then, good judgement is surely one of the key considerations which separates the really successful management from the others.

Protection

The vitally important fact about a competitive advantage is that 'it is an advantage that your competitors do not have'. It is an advantage which is exclusive to the owner (i.e. the operator concerned). This is its great value. If it should become available to others then its value will change, and in all probability the change will be a substantial one. It follows that if you are the owner of a competitive advantage you should take every reasonable action to ensure that it remains your exclusive property for as long as possible.

Wherever possible it is important to take advantage of the protection provided by the law. Patent and copyright law does provide some protection and industries such as pharmaceuticals provide excellent examples of where it has been used most effectively. But in many cases legal protection for a competitive advantage will not be possible and in such cases it will be necessary for the operator (i.e. the owner) to provide his own protection.

If the advantage is for a unit cost based primarily on volume production which is, in turn, dependent on brand leadership, the protection is straightforward – ensure the brand retains its leadership and if possible extends it. If the unit cost advantage is based on a particular manufacturing technique the need will be to ensure the technique and its operation remains strictly confidential.

Production unit costs are often dependent on the conditions and effectiveness of the plant involved. Brand volume may be higher than competitive brands, there may be a very high level of skill present in plant operation, but if the machinery itself is outdated and relatively ineffective, then a competitive advantage based on a superior unit cost is unlikely to survive for long. Protection of the advantage requires the installation of modern, effective plant as rapidly as possible.

The competitive advantage may be the discovery and development of a significant new purpose. When the manufacturer is the first to discover it he is well positioned to make the meeting of this purpose (i.e. the delivery of the particular benefit) his property. If he does this thoroughly, then eventually his brand will become firmly linked with the benefit provision and as others attempt to copy him they could find themselves merely providing his brand with additional publicity. But the manufacturer must take the necessary action to ensure the appropriate link is made with his brand, and he needs to be aware that the time available to him to complete the task may be limited.

With competitive advantages which are relatively insignificant, yet nevertheless of value to the business, the need frequently is to take action to ensure that they are kept as confidential as possible. The rule 'never talk about a development until it has been surpassed by a further advance' has much to recommend it.

Competitive advantages based on special techniques in presentation, particularly advertising presentation, are likely to have only a limited time in which to be effective. They are often difficult to protect; they can be copied rapidly, and their value quickly undermined. However, when a competitive advantage in product performance is linked to an effective special presentation technique, then the product advantage may be enhanced, and as the product and technique are linked then a degree of exclusivity tends to be afforded to the technique.

■ *Competitive advantages are of vital importance to the business. They are difficult to produce. Management has a responsibility to ensure they receive the full available protection – they should not expect this to come by chance, it should be planned for and given the necessary priority in operation.*

The 'Competitive Advantage' Approach for the Total Company

Competitive advantages that feature a product performance advance or a marketing innovation are often quoted. The observer could be forgiven for believing that the competitive advantage concept within the business is for certain levels of management only and not the concern of the 'ordinary' people of the business. If this thought surfaces then it should be quickly dismissed.

A fundamental value of the competitive advantage approach is that it is competitive. It is closely allied to the approach that states 'there is always a better way'. No matter how well the product, or the people of the business, are performing today, there is a better level of performance available. The requirement is to discover the 'better way' ahead of competitors and then to develop and exploit it. If this is done in an effective and efficient manner and on a competitive basis, then the discovery of the 'better way' will have automatically brought into existence the opportunity to develop a competitive advantage.

Of course, specialists such as the chemists in the research and development laboratories, and the marketing managers, have an important part to play in the competitive advantage approach, but the great potential of the rest of the business should certainly not be underestimated.

■ *With good management it should be possible to get every section of the business conscious of the need to find 'a better way' and then to get it into operation and exploited before competitors.*

While the improvements individually may not be of particularly high value, when added together across the whole company they could be of a substantial worth; they could certainly represent a competitive advantage and possibly a significant one.

A Competitive Advantage Alone is not Enough for Success

These notes have emphasized the importance of a competitive advantage, its development and exploitation, in building a successful business. But the heading above is, of course, fully correct: a competitive advantage alone will not bring success.

To play its full part the competitive advantage will need to be built into the company's operations in such a way as to allow its exploitation to make the best possible contribution to the company's progress.

A competitive advantage should always be helpful, but this does not mean that it will be able to turn a loss position into a profit, or automatically propel a brand forward in terms of sales volume and market share. For instance, if Brand B has been allowed to run down in terms of performance and presentation and rests at the bottom of the market, even the introduction of a significant competitive advantage is unlikely to save it, although it may give it some impetus.

Where a competitive advantage has been designed and developed for more general use (as against a specific use) it is always important that care be taken to ensure it is used in the most productive manner. This may possibly mean it should be used on a promising, recently developed, low volume brand rather than with a high volume brand that is in decline.

Ideally a competitive advantage needs to be supported by an effective and efficient business. This way the competitive advantage and the business can work on each other and produce a total result which is above their individual levels.

When a competitive advantage is supported by an inefficient business there is always the danger that it will not be fully exploited, and a competitor will be able to counter with a better operation.

Can a Brand (or a Business) Succeed Without a Competitive Advantage?

So very much here depends on the definition placed on the word 'succeed' and how you measure success.

In the 1970s the concept of the 'Brand Portfolio' received considerable attention. The brands within a business were classified as one of:

- *Stars* – high-share and high-growth brands.
- *Cash Cows* – brands that supply a strong flow of cash.
- *Question Marks* – brands under development that may become stars, or may not.
- *Dogs (or Pets)* – low-share brands that are never likely to make a worthwhile contribution.

In terms of competitive advantage, the 'Star' brands clearly have a competitive advantage; the 'Cash Cows' have had a competitive advantage in the past but it is gradually losing its value; the 'Question Marks' must develop a competitive advantage if they are to advance to be Stars; and the 'Dogs' have never had, or are never likely to have, a competitive advantage.

The very general strategic advice often given to a business that applied the brand portfolio approach was to build your 'Stars', take good care of your 'Cash Cows', sort out your 'Question Marks', and get rid of your 'Dogs'. The advice may be sound in many cases, but if all your brands are 'Dogs' then it is unlikely to be advice you are keen to accept.

The fact is that in many markets, for many of the competitors – and this applies particularly to the smaller companies – all of their brands are likely to be classified as 'Dogs'. Nevertheless, a number of these smaller companies would, by many of the standards normally applied, be considered successful.

They have learnt to live with the 'Dogs'. They have maintained a very tight control of their various indirect costs, and they have extracted all possible gross margin from their relatively small brands. However, it would be wrong to think of the companies that operate without competitive advantages as a successful group. In the main, they struggle to continue in business and would dearly love to have some form of worthwhile competitive advantage.

Competitive Advantage and the 'Added Value' Concept

The concept of 'added value' has received considerable attention in recent years. Some particularly keen advocates of the concept argue that it is the best approach to judging the performance of a business, better than the more widely accepted yardstick of return on capital employed.

A very simple explanation of the concept is to say that added value represents the difference between the cost of input and the value of output. If the cost of input is say £1 and the value of sales (output) is £1.50 then the value added is £0.50. The higher the level of added value, the more successful is the business considered to be.

The 'added value' concept can equally be applied to brands/products marketed by a company. There will be the usual problem of deciding just what is the brand cost (input) but, given that a reasonably accurate figure is available, it should be possible to arrive at a level of added value for each brand/product for a given period of time.

The added value is likely to be close to the level of what is frequently termed as either the 'brand gross margin' or the 'brand contributory margin'. The important figure will be the total for the period, i.e. the unit margin multiplied by the volume.

The strength of the brand's competitive advantage will clearly be a key factor in deciding what level of contributory margin it is likely to reach. A competitive advantage provides a means whereby the operator can offer his customer an 'extra'. He may use this extra to obtain a higher unit price or to go for higher volume. Whichever way he moves he will expect to obtain a higher level of total gross margin with the 'extra' rather than without it. The stronger the competitive advantage, the more attractive is the 'extra', and the higher should be the level of the gross margin.

■ *If you are a keen believer in the 'added value' concept and consider it as a valid measure of the success achieved by your business, then you must surely accept this golden rule and ensure that everyone in the business works to make certain that a significant competitive advantage is built into every one of your brands.*

An acceptance of this golden rule and the approach to business strategy and operations that it requires can have a major impact on a company and on the attitude and performance of the people within it. The competitive advantage concept is essentially competitive. It is directly linked to the approach which reasons "There is always a better way". In particular, it is concerned with providing a brand or product which meets the specific requirements of those customers to whom it is directed more effectively than do competitive brands.

When the people of a business have been persuaded to accept and practise this golden rule they will always be working to improve their performance, and in turn to improve the value of their brands to the customer. They will come to accept that they must be better than competitors in whatever they do – only a superior performance can build a competitive advantage.

Chapter 5

Never Attack the Brand Market Leader Head-on

attack the leader from the flank –
it's safer and cheaper

The golden rule NEVER ATTACK THE BRAND MARKET LEADER HEAD-ON is discussed in Part I of this chapter. Its corollary, ATTACK THE LEADER FROM THE FLANK – IT'S SAFER AND CHEAPER, is considered in Part II.

PART I:
Never Attack the Brand Market Leader Head-on

We need to open the discussion of this golden rule with a short explanation. There can be a market with as many as six major companies all holding market shares of a similar level, say around 12–13%. If one of those companies moves ahead to 13–14% market share it becomes the brand market leader. There can be another market where one company is the brand market leader with a share of say 50%, and the rest of the market is shared on a roughly equal basis by six other companies.

It can be argued that this golden rule applies to all market positions but, as we shall see as the discussion progresses, the reasoning behind it applies very much more clearly in market positions closer to the second one outlined above. Where the market leader has a strong position, as distinct from a marginal one, the golden rule is given a better opportunity to operate.

The Advantages Held by the Strong Brand Market Leader

The main reason why the strong brand market leader is difficult to attack successfully is because his position should provide him with a number of outstanding advantages. Among the more prominent of these advantages are:

1. *A lower unit cost of production.*
   Market leadership (when measured by volume) guarantees a higher volume of production than is available to competitors. This should mean that all the advantages coming from the use of high speed, automated machinery and equipment, should be available to the leader.

   Over recent years, with the further development of computers, and more advanced automation, this advantage has become of even greater significance.

   Of course, the production has to be of a kind where capital equipment and advanced technology can play a key part. The unit cost of production also needs to be of consequence within the total cost.

   In many industries, volume has become a, if not the, key factor in determining product unit production cost.

2. *A lower unit cost of distribution.*
   Here we are concerned firstly with the costs involved in the physical distribution of products. Again it should be possible, with a higher volume level, to obtain a lower unit cost of distribution. However, the physical costs are unlikely to be the most important factor under this heading.

   By far the majority of products/brands use wholesalers and retailers on their way from the manufacturer to the consumer (i.e. the ultimate customer). For their services these traders take a return in the form of the margin they charge.

   Normally, the level of the margin relates to the speed of

turnover of the particular brands concerned. If a brand moves rapidly its percentage margin will be low, and if it is slow moving it will be high.

This can make a major difference to the final selling price. If a retailer buys both Brand A and B for 50p and then takes a margin of 20% on A (a fast moving brand) and 25% on B (a slower moving brand) then the selling prices will be 62.5p for A and 67.0p for B.

This means that Brand A has a significant price advantage over B at the point of sale. In effect Brand A has a saving of 4.5p per unit (a saving on Brand B's price of almost 7%). Clearly this could be very beneficial to sales volume for Brand A, and it is obtained without the incurrence of any direct cost by the manufacturer concerned.

There is one further major advantage that accrues to the brand leader under the distribution heading. Again it is not a direct cost saving but it can be of considerable value.

Larger stores will probably stock most of the brands competing in a particular market. But the smaller and medium-size stores certainly will not. They will stock only a limited number – normally this will include the market leader and a small selection of brands from the top group in the market. And if the very small stores are limited to stocking only one brand then it is likely to be the market leader.

The amount of business in a brand transacted by one small store is unlikely to be of consequence to the manufacturer. But if the position is multiplied by the many thousands of small stores within the market then the total business will certainly be substantial.

The brand leader is clearly in a very strong position to get much more than his 'fair share' of the business transacted in his market through the small, as well as medium-size, stores.

3. *Research and development.*
Established brands need to be kept up-to-date. They may, for instance, need to revise their formula, or to improve their packaging. The market leader's higher volume level will

mean that he can spend more than any other brand in total on research and development and yet have a lower expenditure per unit of sales.

The amount of money spent is not the only factor which brings success in the field of research and development, but it is clearly a factor of considerable importance.

4. *Advertising.*

The brand market leader is able to have a higher total level of advertising for his brand and, as the result of his higher volume, a lower unit cost of advertising.

This means that at any time the leader can achieve a higher level of advertising impact on the consumer than any other brand without spending as much money per unit of sale.

5. *General administration.*

There is no reason why the general costs (e.g. administration, sales force, marketing etc.) of the brand leader should total any more than those of his competitors. Again he should have the advantage of a lower cost per unit of sale.

■ *All of this may seem to be a very good argument for a golden rule which reads 'Build your brand into a market leader, and make sure it stays there'. Given that such a move is a practical one which makes commercial sense, it would indeed be good advice.*

However, we are concerned here with a golden rule which advises against 'attacking the market leader head-on'. Clearly the strong market leader is in a very powerful position. If you decide to attack him you will certainly need to have something very special on your side.

Without this 'something very special' a head-on attack is likely to be costly, risky, and ultimately unsuccessful. This is the basis of the golden rule, and business logic would clearly support it.

Can the Brand Market Leader be 'Taken'?

We are concerned in this section to challenge the golden rule. The market leader has many advantages but, can he be overcome, can he be beaten in the market-place?

The 'key' to beating the market leader rests with the consumer. The consumer must be tempted away from the leading brand and into trying a new or another established brand, and after trying he must be so impressed that he rates this brand as his best value buy and continues to buy it in the future.

The best value concept is now a well-established approach and is featured and discussed in detail as a golden rule earlier in this book. It is based on the very simple fact that whenever a customer makes a purchase he always buys the particular brand or product which, at the time of purchase, represents best value to him.

The concept goes on to reason that for the majority of customers in a wide range of markets there are four 'key' value attributes which go to make up consumer best value. The attributes are:

- *Purpose* – the consumer need the brand meets, or the consumer benefit it provides;
- *Performance* – how well the brand performs in meeting the purpose;
- *Price* – the money the consumer pays for the brand; and
- *Presentation* – the manner and style in which a brand is presented to the consumer.

The brand which wishes to replace the leader must offer better value, and it would be wise to concentrate its efforts on the 'key' attributes within the best value concept.

In fact, the probability of an attacker displacing the market leader can be discussed under the two headings:

1. His own (i.e. the attacker's) actions
2. The actions (or lack of action) of the market leader.

1. The attacker's actions

Here, we are concerned with the ability of the attacker to build a brand or product that has a competitive advantage over the leader, an advantage of such significance that it can become the best value buy of the number of consumers necessary to move it to market leadership.

He may have discovered a new purpose or benefit that has a great attraction for the consumer. Of course, if he wants to displace the market leader the new purpose will need to be directed at the main sector of the market and not a speciality part. A new speciality brand may damage the leader but is unlikely to displace him.

The attacker may also need to be sure that his new purpose is far enough away from that of the leader so that he (the leader) cannot easily assimilate it into his brand.

A new development in formulation or in processing could provide a performance advantage and this may be attractive to the consumer. But if it is to provide the leader with really troublesome competition the advantage will need to be in the 'right' area and of real significance. The record shows very clearly that a marginal advantage, even if it is in the 'right' area, is unlikely to be enough to displace a well established leader. A significant competitive advantage in an aspect of product performance which is of major consequence to the consumer will be necessary.

The attacker can always price his brand below the level of the market leader. If he does not have a significant advantage in performance this will probably be essential. However, a low-price policy is unlikely to be helpful to him unless he has a competitive advantage in product unit cost. This is very unlikely to apply as the market leader will have a much higher volume, and volume is normally a 'key' factor in determining the unit cost level.

If he attempts a price attack and the market leader meets him then the attacker will be in real trouble. He must either reduce his own price further, a move which could be very costly, or lose his brand advantage.

The number of new brands launched on the basis of better presentation (which usually means they believe they have superior advertising) is legion. If this is the only advantage they are able to claim then the record shows that they are very likely to fail.

An outstanding brand presentation can most certainly be a great asset for a brand. But without the right purpose, and the right balance of performance and price, it is unlikely to bring success against the established brand leader.

There can be an exception to this in what are often termed 'emotional' markets (i.e. markets where emotion is considered to be a very strong factor within the buying decision). A market often quoted under this heading is that for perfume.

In emotional markets, brand presentation is always of very special significance. An outstanding presentation could possibly act to dislodge the leader, but even here it would need to be backed by a very good product with a reasonable balance of price and performance.

■ *There are clearly many avenues open to the attacker to explore as he plans to 'take' the brand leader. If he is to succeed he will need to be sure that his brand has a significant competitive advantage in an area of real consequence to appropriate consumers. And, of course, he will need to be sure that he has the necessary operating skills and resources to handle both the attack and the pursuit competently. Possibly most important of all is that he be as sure as is possible that his competitive advantage is big and strong enough to do the job required of it, and that he has the means to give it satisfactory protection.*

Never Attack the Brand Leader Head-on

The U.K. market for washing powders is one of the biggest, and most competitive, of all the U.K. consumer markets. The two major contestants in the market are Lever Bros., a subsidiary company of Unilever, and Procter and Gamble, a subsidiary of Procter and Gamble of the U.S.A.

The Lever brand *Persil*, a soap powder, was the brand market leader through the 1950s, 60s, and 70s. In 1957 P&G mounted a head-on attack on the brand leader when it launched a new soap powder named *Fairy Snow*.

For the brand to have the *Fairy* name was considered to be a great advantage. *Fairy* was the leading brand in the U.K. hard soap market; it had established a high reputation as a product, and also had a very favourable brand personality. (The *Fairy* name was later considered to have been most effective in helping *Fairy Liquid* to the leadership of the U.K. dishwashing liquid market).

Fairy Snow was marketed very skilfully with a strong promotional backing. The brand received extensive advertising support, sampling, special offer packs and store merchandising. *Fairy Snow* was priced at the same level as *Persil*.

Despite the extensive support *Fairy Snow* had only limited success. Through the late 1950s and into the 60s and 70s its market share was generally some 50% below the level of market share held by *Persil*.

Fairy Snow had attacked the market leader head-on and had thereby moved against the golden rule. Despite extensive promotional backing, and the advantages provided by the *Fairy* name, it had recorded only limited success.

In the period 1968/9 Procter and Gamble mounted another head-on attack against *Persil* the brand market leader. This time the attacking brand was named *Ariel*. The brand was marketed skilfully with extensive sampling, advertising, and promotional support. *Ariel* was priced at a premium to *Persil*.

The *Ariel* launch operation was very successful, and for a period the brand moved ahead of *Persil* and into the position of market leader. *Persil* was able to strike back and re-claim its leadership position, but *Ariel* remained a very strong challenger.

This time Procter and Gamble had moved against the 'golden rule' and won. *Ariel* had taken on the brand market leader head-on and had come through with a commendable result.

There was one outstanding difference in the *Fairy Snow* and *Ariel* attacks and it centres on the performance of the product within the brands. *Fairy Snow's* product performance was very similar to that of *Persil*. In certain respects it may have had a marginal advantage, but in other respects it was probably below the *Persil* performance level.

Ariel had a significant competitive advantage in terms of product performance over all other brands in the market at the time of its launch. The *Ariel* formula contained enzyme, a chemical ingredient which has the ability to remove certain difficult stains, including blood, from fabrics in the wash. *Ariel* was the only brand available nationally in the U.K. at this time to have this performance advantage. It was also important that the *Ariel* advantage was one which could be exploited in advertising.

Ariel went against the golden rule, but it had a significant competitive advantage in the 'key' area of performance and this enabled it gain a commendable result. *Fairy Snow* also moved against the golden rule but it did *not* have a competitive advantage in performance and, despite extensive support, and the use of the *Fairy* name, achieved only limited success.

The attacker can also greatly enhance his chances of success by the manner in which he conducts the general management of his business. If he runs an effective and efficient business, one that is lean and able to deliver results, then he clearly has a better chance of success than if his business is ineffective and poorly managed.

His financial position, and the management of his finances, is likely to be of particular importance. A battle with the market leader could well become a lengthy and costly exercise and the attacker needs to be well prepared for this. If he gets it wrong, not only could he lose the particular market-place battle, he could also lose the rest of his business.

2. The actions (or lack of action) of the market leader

How the market leader is behaving is obviously of great significance, and it is appropriate to consider his behaviour under the two headings:

    a. The brand (or brands) concerned
    b. His business in general.

    a. Brands can be managed wisely and actively; they can also be managed unwisely and in an ineffective manner. The brand formula can be allowed to become outdated, its packaging design old fashioned, and its advertising ineffective.

    Against this the brand formula can be kept very much in the lead for performance, and its research and development input maintained at a high level. The design and make-up of its packaging can be reviewed and, as appropriate, adjusted on a regular basis. And its advertising similarly reviewed, and the investment in it maintained at a satisfactory level.

    If the brand is in good shape and well managed then it will obviously be much more difficult to beat. The position is in the hands of the brand leader – only he decides how his brand is managed.

    b. The health and general strength of the market leader's business will have a major influence on the level and quality of resource he is able to place behind his market leading brand. For instance, if the business is desperately short of cash, and not well placed to raise new funds, then any defence expenditure may need to be strictly rationed.

Under this heading should be included the skill and experience of the brand leader's management. This is of very great significance, and if this management is allowed to decline in its level of skill and ability then it will be that much easier for the attacker to make progress.

Clearly of considerable consequence will be the level of skill, and the attitude, of the brand leader's top management. If they are known to be ready to retire, or looking for some other way out of the business, then attacking them should be that much easier.

The question asked at the beginning of this section was "Can the brand market leader be taken?" The answer to this question must clearly be "Yes". Every brand in the market is vulnerable to the 'right' attack. However, it is important that this answer should not be interpreted as a vote against the golden rule.

The brand leader can always be taken, but in practice it very rarely happens as the result of a head-on attack.

This golden rule is very similar to all the others. On rare occasions it may be proven wrong, but in by far the majority of cases it is most certainly correct and represents excellent advice.

As we have already seen, a well-managed brand market leader is in a very strong position, and usually the more dominant his leadership the stronger is his position. To 'take' a strong market leader your brand will need more than just a competitive advantage, it will need a significant competitive advantage. And this advantage will have to be concentrated in an area which is of consequence to consumers. Beyond this you will need skill in planning your strategy, a high level of skill and enthusiasm in your operations, and a satisfactory level of resource backing. And some good fortune will also be helpful. An attack of this kind should be evaluated most carefully before action is taken. The prize for success may be substantial; the cost of failure will also be substantial and it may extend beyond the one brand directly involved.

■ *All of this says that the golden rule 'Never attack the brand market leader head-on' is very sound advice. If you intend to go against it be careful – a number have made the move successfully, but many, many more have failed, and failure can be very expensive.*

How To 'Take' the Market Leader

The U.K. toilet soap market is one of the major toiletry markets in the country, and it is known to be highly competitive. The main contestants in the market in the 1970s (Lever, P&G, and Colgate) were all international companies with very high reputations for their skills in brand marketing. However, in the 1970s/and early 1980s the brand leadership of the market was 'taken' twice.

There are basically two ways in which the brand market leader can be 'taken'. One way is a 'head-on' attack (which is against the golden rule), and the other way is to make an attack from an established flank position. Both approaches feature in the 'takeover' operations in the toilet soap market.

In the early 1970s the market was dominated by a limited number of well-established brands. *Lux* toilet soap, *Palmolive*, and *Lifebuoy* toilet soap had all been in existence for over 40 years. *Camay* had been introduced in the 1950s and *Fairy* toilet soap in the 1960s.

Positioned some 3–4 points below the leading group was the *Imperial Leather* brand. Owned by the Cussons Company, it was sold as a luxury soap and at a premium price. The brand had a well-developed and favourable personality. *Imperial Leather* was, in effect, a well-positioned flanking brand.

In 1975 the Cussons Company was purchased by Paterson Zochonis – *Imperial Leather* had new owners.

In 1976 Lever launched a brand named *Shield* into the market. Originally developed as a specialty brand, *Shield* had received such an enthusiastic reception from consumers that it was re-positioned and in its national launch was aimed directly at market leadership. It was outstandingly successful and did indeed achieve market leadership immediately after its launch.

For *Shield*, its product quality, highly acceptable fragrance, design, packaging, and presentation had all worked together to give the brand a significant competitive advantage over all the other brands available in the market. This advantage had enabled *Shield* to go against the golden rule and yet still achieve the leading position in the market. The brand had demonstrated that if your competitive advantage is strong enough and your operation skilfully managed you can 'take' the leader head-on.

The new owners of *Imperial Leather,* possibly impressed by the progress of the *Shield* brand, saw a marketing opportunity for their brand. *Imperial Leather* received much stronger advertising and promotional support; it engaged in trade dealing and in this way its price premium was reduced, and it received stronger in-store merchandising support.

The brand reacted very favourably to this new approach and soon became a member of the leading group of brands within the market, and later the holder of the No. 1 position as market leader.

Imperial Leather's price premium had been reduced without officially cutting its price, and its well-developed 'luxury' personality had been maintained despite the heavier promotional activity. The brand's move is a good example of how the very difficult task of 'taking' the leader from the flank can be achieved.

The *Shield* and *Imperial Leather* operations were both helped by the fact that the U.K. toilet soap market at this time had no one dominant brand leader. The attacking brands did not have to cope with a leader who was armed with the advantages that dominance brings.

PART II
Attack the Leader from the Flank – it's Safer and Cheaper

This statement is often quoted as a form of corollary to the golden rule which is discussed in Part I. It is considered here as a separate statement as there are a number of special factors concerned with its operation which are worthy of study. Firstly, it is necessary to consider the wording of the statement because it can be misleading.

While it is true that all brands in a particular market are in some degree of competition with each other, an attack on the 'flank' would not necessarily be considered an attack on the leader. In fact, should a new brand enter, for instance, the premium sector of a market with a speciality appeal and promise, it is unlikely to have more than a marginal effect on the leader.

If the statement is referring to the establishment of a brand in a market where there is a dominant leader then, as we shall see later in the discussion, this should be a much easier task if the brand is directed toward a speciality position (i.e. the flank) rather than at the main market sector.

Beyond this, it could be argued that the statement really means "Build a position on the flank with a view to attacking the leader at a later date". An approach of this kind could have much to recommend it, but it is of course a very different proposition.

The Advantages of Establishing a Brand in a 'Flank' Position

The 'flank' position will be outside the main sector of the market. Its volume and revenue is likely to be very much lower than the main sector, and the competition within it should be more limited. It follows that a well-directed, and well-managed, attack on the 'flank' position should have a better chance of success than would an attack on the main sector.

Many of the disadvantages of attacking head-on will be avoided by a flanking movement, and the market leader will need to be careful if he decides to take any action. If he (the leader) attempts to meet the special benefit then he may well confuse his present users and this could prove costly.

The valuable volume advantages possessed by the leader in the main sector may not be of the same significance when the special sector is considered. For instance, one of the advantages of volume should be a lower unit cost of production which in turn can mean a lower sales price. In the special 'flanking' sector there could be an established premium price position in operation and the need to meet the leader's lower price may not apply.

Similarly there can be advantages in advertising. The advertising promise for a speciality brand can be distinctive. It could be the only such promise in the market, and again it does not have to compete directly with the leader.

The speciality appeal could also help in making a lower level of advertising investment do a satisfactory job. It could be possible to avoid some of the very popular, but relatively expensive, media and to concentrate on less costly media that have a special attraction for the targeted users.

Advantages are also present in dealing with the wholesale and retail trade. The speciality brand will be placed in position on the shelves as a speciality; it will not be positioned directly alongside the leader. And it is unlikely to have to fight for the same display and feature space as the leader.

The trade will probably expect to take a higher level of percentage unit margin for the speciality brand, but the manufacturer can allow for this in his pricing, and he may possibly be able to make it an attraction to the trade.

Is a 'Flanking' Operation Sure to be Safer?

It is necessary to define just what we mean by 'safer' in this context. If by safer we really mean successful then the answer should be "Yes" in by far the majority of cases. In the earlier part of this chapter we have considered why a head-on attack is likely to be a failure, and in this section we have covered the advantages of 'flanking'. From this it is clear that if we mean successful in terms of establishing a brand in the market then the flanking operation is more likely to be safer.

If the term safer is related to the investment in the operation and its ability to return a reasonable level of profit, then again the answer must be "Yes". A financial success is clearly linked to the market success.

If we are concerned with introducing a brand that will challenge the leader for his position then the answer is more difficult. As we have seen, there will be occasions when this can be achieved by a head-on attack if the attacker has a significant competitive advantage and/or the leader has allowed his management to become ineffective. But these occasions must be classified as very special occasions.

Changing a specialist brand into a challenger for market leadership is discussed later in this chapter. As we shall see, it is most certainly not a simple operation.

Is a 'Flanking' Operation Sure to be Cheaper?

We need to begin by defining what we mean by 'cheaper' in this context. If we mean cheaper in terms of the sum of money to be invested, then the answer must be "Yes, in the majority of cases". The attack on a specialist sector of the market is likely to be a much smaller operation, the actual outlay on the initial promotional and advertising moves will be lower, and the investment in such items as product stock also considerably lower. However, if we take a longer term view and include any expenditures that may be necessary to convert a specialist brand into a challenger for market leader, then the total may not be cheaper. Much will depend on how the challenge is mounted.

Of course, if we define cheaper in terms of the effect of the operation on the profit level of the business then the 'flanking' operation should certainly be the clear winner over the shorter term. It is much more likely to produce a successful brand. But again, if we look longer term then it becomes much more difficult to provide a clear answer. The question is now really one of which approach is likely to produce a successful brand that can 'take' the market leader, and we know that for both approaches this is a very difficult objective to achieve. For both, the probability of failure is high, although the likelihood of success probably favours the flanking move.

Developing and Launching a Successful 'Flanking' Brand

When this particular golden rule is discussed the statement 'launch a flanking brand' is often made in a casual manner which implies that this is a very simple task. In fact, of course, it is far from a simple task; indeed, it is a very difficult one.

In elementary terms, the first three steps in an outline for a 'flanking' brand marketing success would read:

- Find the marketing opportunity (i.e. the consumer need or benefit not served adequately by an existing brand). Assess and evaluate it.
- Define the competitive advantage necessary to exploit the opportunity.
- Decide whether or not you are able to develop, and then exploit, the competitive advantage more effectively, and more rapidly, than your competitors.

These are, of course, the three initial steps for the development of any new brand, irrespective of where it is to be positioned in the market. When they have been negotiated successfully the task of actually developing the opportunity, and in particular the competitive advantage, has to be carried through. This is certainly not an easy exercise. The record makes this very clear. It is a difficult operation, and the failures far outweigh the successes.

Much will depend on the particular market. "Is it in its growth stage?' or 'Has it moved through to maturity or decline?" If the market has reached maturity then the task of finding a new marketing opportunity will be that much more difficult.

The competitors operating in the market will also be of consequence. We have already noted that the level of managerial effectiveness will be a major consideration. New brand introduction into a 'sleepy' market is likely to be a much easier task than one into a 'live' market where active and effective managements are in operation. If the new brand is to eventually have the ability to overtake the market leader then the task is even more difficult.

If the brand has been directed at a small speciality sector, then, even if it is highly successful, it is unlikely to be able to make the transition to the main sector and market leadership. For instance, if the market leader has say a 30% share, then a speciality brand that may be considered successful and satisfactorily profitable with, say,

3% is unlikely ever to be able to make a move for leadership that will be considered as a serious challenge.

■ *As a very general rule, if a flanking brand is to make a serious challenge against the leader it will need to be positioned with a reasonably well-accepted benefit, and to hold a market share which is at least half of that of the leader.*

Flanking on 'Price'

When 'flanking' is discussed, the possibility of using a flanking attack against the brand leader based on a lower price is invariably very high on the list of approaches under consideration. The reasoning tends to go along the lines that if a brand could be launched with a benefit very similar to that of the leader, with a formula which delivers a very close performance match, but with a lower unit price, it must have a very good chance of success. If a 'clever' advertising campaign can be added then the probability of success must be even higher.

This reasoning has many weaknesses. First, if the challenger has a similar performance level to that of the leader then he will probably have a unit cost which is the same or slightly higher than that of the leader. From such a position an attack on price could prove very expensive and there is no guarantee of success.

It must be appreciated that the record shows that the challenger will need more than a marginal price advantage. If the price differential is to get home to consumers it will need to be of significance. Beyond this the leader may well decide to meet the price challenge in the shorter term. This will mean the challenger will need to make a further costly cut.

■ *A price move can work when the leader has followed a high-margin policy and for some particular reason is either unable or unwilling to reduce his margin (in effect, unable or unwilling to change his price).*

It can also work where the challenger has developed a means whereby he can obtain a significantly lower unit cost of production for his product. This should give him the opportunity to apply a significant price advantage.

It will be most important for any challenger who proposes to use price as his main weapon of attack to be sure of his own financial position and also to have a shrewd knowledge of that of the leader. A price challenge can often mean that both contestants are forced into a lengthy period of expensive operations, and the one with the deepest pocket may well become the eventual winner.

In a market where the leader has held his price at a premium level to cover the cost of a product that is of a higher quality than is required by a large section of his consumers, then he can be vulnerable. In effect, the challenger will be able to create a new market sector, and it could be one that is ultimately bigger than that dominated by the leader. The challenger has another advantage here – the leader may find it difficult to change his own quality level as many of his loyal customers will have become accustomed to it.

It is always possible that a 'flanking' operation based on a higher price than the leader will prove a better position for a successful attack. The higher price would need to be accompanied with a suitably higher quality, and the attacker would need to give his brand a favourable personality. Into the future he may be able to attack the leader and include a price reduction in this attack. This approach can be particularly attractive where the challenger has an effective management, one that has a higher level of performance than the leader, and where he can obtain cost reductions in his brand formula and operations. Of course, the attacking brand would need a reasonable level of market share from which to start its attack.

Developing a 'Flanking' Brand into a Market Leader – the Task and the Risk

We have already given this subject limited consideration in the paragraphs above. It is clearly not a simple move to make; indeed, it would normally be a most difficult one to complete successfully. While there are a number of examples where it has been accomplished, there are many more where it has failed.

Often the challenger will be involved in making a change in his brand purpose (i.e. the benefit or consumer need it meets). This is a notoriously difficult move to make and one with which there must always be considerable risk. For instance, can the consumer be tempted to try, and accept, that a toilet soap he has acknowledged as a deodorant is now also a soft and creamy beauty bar? Or will he become confused?

■ *The possibility of causing consumer confusion is probably the greatest risk. There is always the danger that the successful speciality brand will fail to make the transition to the main sector, and simultaneously lose its position as a speciality. Such a failure is doubly expensive – the profit contribution could fall and the attempt to change will have been costly.*

The development whereby the speciality brand is prepared to narrow, or possibly remove, its price differential is normally accompanied by a lower degree of risk. Frequently the narrowing can be carried out primarily by promotional moves (e.g. extensive sampling operations).

For the speciality brand to obtain the necessary level of volume increase that the attack will need for success it is normally important that its purpose (its benefit) is one that is already fully acceptable to the main sector consumer (e.g. when the brand's benefit is a very high level of performance, namely, higher than the market leader).

Attack the Leader From the Flank – It's Safer and Cheaper

Within the total U.K. household cleaning market the market for scourers was always of importance. In the early 1960s it totalled approximately. 60,000 tons in volume. Two brands dominated the market – *Ajax* (Colgate/Palmolive) which was the clear market leader, with a brand share of approximately. 60%, and *Vim* (Lever) which had a share of some 35%.

Through the late 1960s and early 1970s Lever put considerable effort behind *Vim* and the brand made good progress. But although *Vim* began to challenge *Ajax,* at times getting to within 4 – 5 points of the leader, it never managed to overtake the Colgate brand.

Lever decided it had to find another way to take over the leadership of the scourer market. A head-on attack against *Ajax* in the powder market would have been against the golden rule and had no attraction.

Marketing research was beginning to record complaints from consumers that the powder scourers – *Ajax* and *Vim* – were guilty of scratching the new plastic surfaces which were starting to appear in kitchens and bathrooms throughout the U.K.

Lever had tested a liquid 'non-scratch' bathroom cleaner in a U.K. region and it had performed reasonably well. This product was adapted for use in the kitchen, bathroom, and other areas. It required a plastic container and needed to retail at a price considerably higher than the powder products. However, it was attractive to many consumers and certainly had potential for the future as the use of plastic in the kitchens and bathrooms became more widespread.

Lever moved into the U.K. national market in 1974 with its new liquid product, the brand name was *Jif*. It was a flanking attack, but it had in view that one day, in the longer term, *Jif* could make an attack to become brand market leader.

For a number of years *Jif* grew steadily within the market. By 1980 the number of households in the U.K. buying liquid scourers was close to the number buying powder products. By 1982 *Jif* had moved into clear brand market leadership, comfortably outselling *Ajax*.

Lever had obeyed the golden rule, it had *not* attacked the brand market leader head-on. It had built a brand – *Jif* – on the flank which was clearly an easier and less expensive move. It had ultimately used the brand on the flank to move into the main market and to attack the market leader successfully. *Jif* was, of course, helped by the developments in the market.

This had been a 'textbook' operation for Lever – *Jif* went on to strengthen its market position, increase its volume, and to become an outstanding brand in the U.K. household cleaner market.

In considering this golden rule we have accepted the lead statement NEVER ATTACK THE BRAND MARKET LEADER HEAD-ON.

The many advantages which accrue to the market leader mean that his position should be an extremely strong one. Providing that he manages his brand and business effectively he should be able to repel a head-on attack and inflict very considerable damage on the attacker.

As with all the golden rules NEVER ATTACK THE BRAND MARKET LEADER HEAD-ON is basically right and should be treated with respect. The corollary to this golden rule which has been discussed in Part II requires further definition before it can gain acceptance as a golden rule.

If we are concerned with establishing a worthwhile brand in a market which has a dominant leader, then it should be both safer and cheaper to introduce a 'flanking' brand (i.e. a brand which has a specialist appeal, and avoids the main sector of the market and direct competition with the leader).

Here the corollary is 'basically correct' and should be respected as a golden rule. However, a speciality brand is unlikely to make a big impression on the dominant market leader; the launch of the speciality brand is unlikely to be considered as an 'attack' by the leader.

To launch a 'flanking' brand with the intention of later, when it is well established, moving it into the main sector and attacking the leader is an approach which has been known to be successful. But it is an extremely difficult operation requiring a particularly high level of skill and application in brand development.

■ *If the brand market leader is to be 'taken' there would seem to be three basic requirements. First, the development of a significant competitive advantage and one that lends itself to effective exploitation. Second, the attacker's business needs to be skilfully managed. And third, he needs to be sure he has adequate resources to carry through his attack and the pursuit which will need to follow.*

Chapter 6

If You're Not Going to Win, Don't Play

only winners can expect to survive and prosper

It is highly probable that at some time during their school days youngsters in the United Kingdom will have been advised by their schoolmasters that the important rule is to "Play the game, enjoy it, and not
to worry too much about the result". The same advice is probably
given by masters at schools throughout the many other sports-loving
countries of the world.

We must remember that the schoolmasters are referring to sport,
and in particular amateur sport. Their advice is well founded. For the
amateur sportsman the important consideration is the physical exercise, the enjoyment of the occasion, and the development of the right
spirit and approach.

Should the youngsters carry their masters' advice forward into the
world of business, they could soon be in trouble. By all means enjoy
your business – it may well provide excellent training and exercise for
the mind – but never forget that in business winning is all important.
In business, only the winner can expect to receive a big prize; for other
competitors there may be no prize at all. Only the winner can expect
to survive and prosper; for the losers there may be no future.

At one time the leaders of business in the U.K. were strongly
criticized because they were thought to be too heavily influenced by
the teachings of the masters in the established schools. 'Playing the

game' was considered to be very important. Losing was certainly not a disgrace; indeed, if 'losing after putting up a good fight' was the position then it could possibly rate as a first class performance.

The shrewd businessman would, of course, have questioned whether or not it was wise to have entered the particular market, and also whether the business should have allowed itself to be drawn into the fight. He may well have decided to have 'sold out' as he saw the possibility of a fight approaching.

■ *Over more recent years there has been a wide appreciation that while the school teachings may have much to recommend them in the training and development of young people, they do not all have a direct transfer to the world of business. Some of the teachings are just not suitable for business. Acceptance of this position is of significance, and means that this golden rule is worthy of repetition, "In business, IF YOU'RE NOT GOING TO WIN, DON'T PLAY".*

The Basis for this Golden Rule and Why it Should be Followed

There was at one time considerable discussion as to the basis for this golden rule. However, there now appears to be general agreement that the rule is based on market-place performance.

■ *It is a fact that a very large majority of consumer product companies, and similar facts apply in the industrial and service sectors, make the bulk of their profit from those markets where their brands hold a commanding share position. Taking this one stage further, it is also a fact that the dominant brand leader of a market is invariably the brand which makes the major part of the profit generated within that particular market. The stronger the leadership the bigger the profit earning differential between the leader and the other competing brands. Under this golden rule winning is associated with brand market leadership, preferably a dominant leadership, and there is good business economic backing for this.*

If your brand is No. 1 in a market then it should be the leading profit producer. Much will depend on the extent of the leadership. Only the clear leader can expect to have a markedly superior position to his competitors.

Should your brand be No. 2 then it is likely to be, in part, dependent on the leader's approach for its level of profit. If the leader takes a low margin approach then the second brand will be forced to follow this and his profits will be limited. If the leader is prepared to operate a form of price umbrella then the second and other brands in the market may be able to fare better; but they will still need to keep a very wary eye on the leader.

For the third and fourth brands in the market the position is sure to be much more difficult. Their profit level is likely to be limited, even where the leader is prepared to provide a price umbrella, where the leader operates on low margins, their profits will be at a very low level and possibly non-existent.

These remarks apply where the leader is strong with a volume of, say, some 30% or more ahead of the second brand. Where the leader has only a small lead (e.g., say, 2 or 3%), then the position changes. He (the leader) is unlikely to be able to act in a dominant manner and will need to be more fully aware of the actions of his competitors.

The remarks also require that the leader be efficient in his operations. If you are leader and you are efficient, then the greater your lead, the stronger your position. However, if you are inefficient, then the competitive advantage that your volume should bring you in terms of unit production and distribution costs could well become a marked disadvantage.

■ *All this really adds to the golden rule and says "If you are not going to win, and win in a dominant manner, don't play".*

Winning and Profit

One of the main criticisms of this particular golden rule is that it fails to provide any form of clear and precise definition of what it means by the term 'win', and it does not mention profit. It has already been stated that it is now generally accepted that the reference is to market-place performance. However, many businessmen would point out that the objective of a business organization is profit and this golden rule appears to ignore this. They would argue that profit should be linked to winning within the rule.

We have already considered the fact that a strong market leadership position should lead to good profitability, but it has to be accepted that market leadership and profit do not necessarily go together. It is always possible, though a very rare happening, for the third or fourth brand in a market to make more profit than the leader.

The golden rules are all relatively simple statements. This simplicity is one of the reasons why they are remembered and quoted. No doubt they were originated by practical people and are founded on long experience. They are not likely to have come from the academic world where detailed and more qualified definitions are developed.

If we try to link the winning directly with profit, then we are quickly into the world of 'how much profit', and then on to 'return on capital employed', and so forth.

It can be argued that if a manufacturer sees an opportunity in a market to launch a brand entrant which will go on to hold the second or third place, and he is very confident that it can return a satisfactory level of profit, then he should go ahead and launch it. Given that the operation is successful it should earn a level of profit that will provide an acceptable return on the investment it requires. Surely, this is winning.

Much will depend on the level of return achieved and on the alternative investments open to the business. Beyond this the security of the second or third position (particularly the third position) and its dependence on the attitude and behaviour of the leader, will always be important considerations.

■ *What this golden rule is telling you to do, should you be presented with a proposal that reasons in terms of a lower level market position, is to go back to the managers responsible for the proposal, and to challenge them to use their skills to find a better investment for your money. Don't accept the risks associated with second or third place; if you really apply your skills you can do better. You can produce a winner, a leader, if you are skilful and prepared to work hard enough. And so very often this is good advice.*

The position of the speciality or 'niche' brand is somewhat different. Here the golden rule requires it to be a winner in its speciality section. This could mean that in terms of the total market it is placed say fifth or sixth. However, leadership of its speciality should enable it to take a suitable premium price and a reasonable level of profit. A second or third position in the speciality is unlikely to return a satisfactory profit position.

There can be exceptional occasions when a manufacturer has an objective other than market share or profit for a brand over the shorter term. It is possible for circumstances to apply whereby a new brand is launched specifically to stop a competitive brand. Its market share gain may be small and its profit contribution very low, but if it succeeds in stopping the competitive brand then it will have been successful. In the eyes of its owner the brand will be rated as a winner. However, it has to be accepted that brands of this kind are very exceptional.

Should it be "If You're Not Going to Achieve Your Objective, Don't Play"?

Part of the reasoning in the heading above is clearly moving toward changing this golden rule and including a reference to objectives and their achievement rather than to winning. Would this be a wise move?

The golden rules are simple statements and they do have weaknesses. However, making alterations which move away from simplicity should be avoided, and a move to 'objectives' would surely be a move away from simplicity. It would also bring with it further problems.

To have a meaning the objective would need to be specified with clarity. If it is to be profit contribution then how much and in what time period? If it is to be stopping a competitor then again the measure and the time period would need to be specified, and in this case a clear specification would be especially difficult.

What if the objective is set at 'too easy' or 'too difficult' a level? The old cynical story of budgets comes to mind. Within the business the important battle to win is the one which sets your budget level. If you win and get a good level you will have a peaceful year, if you lose and get a low level your year will be one of constant pressure.

To Play and Achieve the Objective – But Not To Win

In 1968 Procter & Gamble launched a new brand named *Ariel* into a regional test within the U.K. washing powder market. At the time the clear brand leader of the market was the Lever brand *Persil.*

The *Ariel* brand formula contained an enzyme, a chemical ingredient which had special performance abilities in the removal of certain stains, including blood, from fabrics in the wash. At this time *Ariel* was the only brand in the U.K. market to offer this benefit and it represented a significant competitive advantage.

In 1969 *Ariel* completed its national introduction and quickly replaced *Persil* as the brand market leader.

Persil was a vitally important brand to Lever in the U.K. As the leader in one of the U.K.'s biggest consumer markets it was a very significant profit contributor. Beyond this, *Persil* was the company's 'flagship' brand and had a major part to play in its relationship with its direct customers (the U.K. grocery trade), and in building and maintaining morale within the company. Lever had to get *Persil* back to market leadership.

The Lever chemists were able to produce a product formula which would perform at a similar level to that of *Ariel.* However, they were not able to provide a competitive advantage in performance; to do this they required additional time.

Given this position Lever decided not to attempt an immediate re-staging of the *Persil* brand. Nevertheless, the *Ariel* threat to Lever had to be faced. If this P&G brand was allowed to proceed without a direct challenge it could establish a leadership position which even a re-staged *Persil* would have difficulty in countering.

Lever decided to combat the *Ariel* attack with a two brand approach. *Persil* was to move immediately into a very strong defensive programme using theme advertising and extensive promotions. A new brand named *Radiant* was to be launched into the market as a direct competitor to *Ariel.* The aim was that *Radiant* should be successful in its own right, but most importantly it should stop, and then regress, the development of *Ariel.* At a later date (hopefully within a reasonably short time period) *Persil* was to be re-staged with a new product formulation which would justify it going back to the consumer for re-sampling.

This Lever approach carried considerable risk, and two points were of particular significance. The first concerned the ability of the Lever chemists to produce an appropriate development for the *Persil* formula within a reasonable time period. The second was linked to the price of *Radiant*. Lever was convinced this new brand needed to be priced below the *Ariel* level; but it was always possible that P&G would reduce the price of *Ariel*, and this would mean that *Radiant* would have to go lower. At an even lower price the *Radiant* operation could have been extremely costly.

The launch of *Radiant* did make a major contribution to the stopping of *Ariel*, and it also helped to provide *Persil* with a suitable time period for re-staging.

When the reformulated *Persil* entered the market the brand was able to recover market leadership. *Ariel* continued as a strong competitor but *Persil* was back again in the No. 1. position.

The Lever strategy had worked reasonably well. The Lever chemists had produced a new *Persil* formulation in good time; *Ariel* did not reduce its price; *Radiant* had a limited (but very valuable) success; and *Persil* was restored to the position of clear brand market leader.

It can be argued that with the *Radiant* brand operation Lever had moved against the golden rule IF YOU'RE NOT GOING TO WIN – DON'T PLAY. Lever did not expect *Radiant* to beat *Ariel* in terms of market share – in this respect it did not believe it would win. Nevertheless Lever went ahead and 'played' with the brand. But Lever did achieve its main objective, and *Radiant* played its full part.

Lever had moved against the golden rule and had come out with a reasonable result, but the circumstances were most exceptional and the risks very high.

How Can You Be Sure You Will Win?

The very simple answer to this question is that in any business activity you can never be sure of the outcome, you can never be absolutely sure you will win. It follows that if you obeyed this golden rule to the letter you would never enter a new business venture. Of course, the rule should not be taken literally. However, it does require that you make appropriate assessments and evaluations before entry.

What are appropriate assessments? Clearly they will vary from case to case. For the launch of a new brand into a relatively new market they could be most extensive. They would certainly include a detailed assessment of the market and its development, a thorough testing and assessment of the proposed new brand, and an evaluation of the competitors and their likely actions. The assessments must be followed by a realistic evaluation, in particular an evaluation of the 'competitive advantage' the operator expects to bring to the venture.

For the small operator the assessment may not necessarily involve computer programmes and other highly detailed considerations, but nevertheless it will need to be carried out with the same level of skill and realism. For both large and small businesses the actual operational planning, and the skill and effort applied in 'making it happen', will be of great significance.

Probably the most important consideration is that your plans and objectives should be realistic. Very ambitious plans for market growth should be questioned closely. Thoughts that unit prices will be maintained when the market grows, and that competitors will not use price to retaliate, should also be questioned closely. The idea that competitors will withdraw meekly should be reviewed – in real life it rarely happens. Competitors usually make every effort to hang on, and sometimes they prove to be very good at it.

You can never be 'completely sure' you will win, but you can make a realistic assessment of your position and your chances. You can get a realistic view of the risks involved. Very importantly you should be able to get a realistic view of the 'downside' risk involved in the venture. This will indicate how much you stand to lose if all goes wrong – in effect, just how much of your whole business could be in danger.

■ *Whether or not you move ahead with a proposition is your decision. The judgement is yours. You can if you wish accept a high-risk proposition. You can decide to disregard this golden rule. But if you do, you should be aware of what is involved for the project and for the whole business if the golden rule proves to be right. And if you are not as sure as is reasonably possible that you will win, a further review of the proposition could be appropriate.*

The Time Period

Over what time period should the project be judged? Is it necessary that the new brand should 'win' within three years, or would ten years be a satisfactory period?

The time period should be one that represents a satisfactory business proposition for the operator concerned. Normally the project would be expected to make an acceptable rate of return on the resources invested in it over a time period that experience has shown to be a reasonable one for the type and form of project involved.

To spend excessive sums of money to 'buy' leadership without any real regard to profitability is clearly not acceptable. This is a return to the need to meet the business objectives which must ultimately be linked to profit making. Of course, it is always possible that a project may in itself be unprofitable and yet benefit the total business effort. Such projects tend to be limited in number and clearly require special consideration.

High-risk Operations

Following this particular golden rule would appear to forbid the acceptance for operation of a high-risk proposition. And yet almost every successful business has at least one brand or project that it points to with some pride purely because it was a high-risk operation that was nursed through successfully and is now a star performer.

The first observation to make is that the same successful businesses are unlikely to mention the many high-risk operations they have had which have failed and have been very costly to the business.

It can be argued that every business should have a high-risk project within its portfolio of operations. However, the high-risk project should not be the only one. The core of the business operations should be projects that follow the lead of the golden rule; they should be projects with which the business has every confidence that it is going to win. Only when it has a sufficient number of 'win' projects should it begin to consider those with high risk. If the balance should change and the 'high risk' outnumber the 'win' projects then the position of the business could be in danger. It follows that 'high-risk' projects are much more likely to fail – and project failure can be very expensive. Failing more than once could well threaten the future of the entire business.

It is important that the manufacturer should be sure what is the 'top side' level of resource that is at risk with a 'high-risk' project. Beyond this he should satisfy himself that the level of return he is to receive if the project is successful is a high one – only if the prospective return is an exceptional one is such a project worth considering.

■ *One of the major problems often associated with 'high-risk' projects is that they are invariably attractive in terms of management challenge. They are interesting and managers, particularly senior managers, see them as a stimulating challenge to their intellect. They become great consumers of management time – for instance, the board spends 75% of its time trying to rescue the 'high-risk' project, and then crams the whole of the 'bread and butter' business into the remaining 25%. Soon the basic business begins to suffer.*

'High-risk' projects should be most carefully controlled. They should not be allowed to become 'hobby' projects for senior managers and thereby exempted from the financial and other disciplines which would normally apply. However, there can of course be a place for 'high-risk' projects in the portfolio of the business. They need to be limited in number, and limited in terms of the resource they are to consume, well controlled, and their potential return should be high enough to recompense for the level of risk involved.

Projects Already in the Market

The comments on this golden rule within this chapter have tended to concentrate on projects which are at a stage of development prior to the actual investment of resources, or certainly before the investment of any extensive resources. This is an understandable approach as the golden rule is intended to apply to new projects and, in particular, new brands. Does it also apply to projects where investment has already been made, or to projects that have been in the market for a period? There is a very great difference from an investment viewpoint between a project that is in the planning stage (without actual investment) and one where investment has commenced.

When the consideration is uncommitted resources (i.e. a project before investment is made) it is always possible to withdraw and to direct the resources to alternative projects. This can be done without loss except that certain preliminary expenses may have been incurred. However, if resources have been committed, (i.e. investment has been made in the project) then the requirement will be to make the best of the position.

If the project has gone badly wrong the best move may be to withdraw completely. This means either selling the project intact, or selling the equipment etc. piecemeal. Should the project be partially successful then the most beneficial move could be to continue with it for a period before arranging to sell.

With a project that clearly has good potential if certain relatively simple shorter term problems are corrected then the best course of action could be to continue with the investment as originally planned. In these circumstances the operator will be obliged to play even if he is forced to face the fact that, certainly in the shorter term, he is unlikely to 'win'.

In the assessment and decision making which should apply in circumstances where the operator has already made an investment, or series of investments, the golden rule has a part to play. If he is not going to 'win' then the operator is likely to obtain, at best, only a limited return on his investment. The big return will go to the winner.

■ *It is important that he should be fully conscious of this in reaching his decision for action, in particular in reaching his strategic decision. He needs to be realistic in deciding whether or not he can get into a position to challenge for leadership (i.e. to win). And if he cannot see his way clear for leadership he needs to be very sure that a position at a lower level will be worthy of the effort and investment it may require.*

As we have already seen, if the brand cannot rise above the fourth or fifth place then it will probably make a 'full cost' loss. And even in second or third place it may struggle to return a satisfactory level of profit.

In the opening paragraphs of this chapter reference was made to the fact that in school it is highly probable that the importance of 'playing the game' irrespective of the result would be emphasized. It is also probable that the requirement that you 'play hard to the final whistle even when you are losing' was also stressed. Considerations such as school pride, team spirit, and personal pride would also feature prominently in the school approach.

In business the reasoning may need to be very different. If it is right to move out of a project then frequently it will be advisable to get out as soon as possible and not to be concerned about 'playing hard to the final whistle'. And the experienced and skilful operator will certainly not allow pride, either company or personal, to get in the way of a withdrawal at the 'right' time, and that may mean a very rapid withdrawal.

Defining the Market

Having accepted that this golden rule is concerned with 'winning' in terms of market leadership it becomes of major importance to be sure that we have defined the market concerned correctly. The important question to be answered is 'Leadership of exactly which market?'

With which other products is the brand in competition? Which other products are alternatives in the view of the customer? Is margarine a competing product with butter in the view of the consumer? Or is there a distinct butter market and also a separate margarine market?

These are questions of great significance. There is likely to be only limited value in being leader of a margarine market if, in the view of the customer, butter and margarine are fully interchangeable, and butter brands completely dominate the total position. In these circumstances, for real success it is likely to be necessary to win in the total market (i.e. both butter and margarine).

Markets tend to move up and down; they certainly never remain completely static. Customer needs and requirements are changing all the time and at some period a particular change can become of significance. For instance, as customers become more and more health conscious the demand for special kinds of margarine may grow and become independent of butter. Leadership of this new margarine market could be a very worthy target and one in which to 'win' could prove highly profitable.

A market where time has been of consequence in determining its make-up is that for toilet soaps. At one time many people used hard soap for personal washing and the sale of toilet soap was very limited. During this period, for many considerations, it was appropriate to consider toilet and hard soaps as forming one soap market.

As people became more affluent and their personal needs changed so the use of toilet soap grew and very little hard soap was used for personal washing. At this time there was clearly a distinct toilet soap market.

Over recent periods, with an even higher level of affluence, the requirements of consumers have again been changing. Now a series of creams, oils, and lotions are beginning to compete directly with toilet soaps. Already there is a need in certain instances to consider the market for toilet soaps and these various cleansing creams etc. as one.

It is important to be sure of the geographical spread of the market. Is there a market for Scotland, or is it an integral part of the total U.K. market? Factors of this kind are clearly of great significance when considerations such as potential production volumes and unit costs need to be forecast.

Recent periods have seen the breakdown of many national borders and the growth of a wider international approach; the development of the Single European Market is a good example of this. In some cases it will remain correct to reason in terms of a national market (e.g. for the U.K.), and the requirement will be to 'win' in this market. But in other cases the movement of product across national borders may be at a very high level. Here the need may well be to reason in terms of the total European market.

With brands that have a 'specialist' appeal there is a need to be sure of the current size and probable development of the market sector in which they compete. Is the 'specialist' sector clearly separated from the main market or is there considerable overlap with a number of major brands in part covering the speciality? In a distinct market sector, leadership of the sector would be a 'win'. But where the sector is overlapped by the main market, leadership is unlikely to bring the same cost benefits over competitors or provide the same pricing opportunity.

■ *The definition of the market is clearly a most important factor in the application of this golden rule. The operator should be concerned to include all the brands/products that are intended to meet the same consumer benefit. He may be justified in treating certain of the minority brands as being part of a speciality sector, and he may need to vary his decision over time and as the market develops. He should certainly not exclude brands/products merely because they are not manufactured locally.*

[**Note**: The whole question of the market and its definition is considered in further detail in the discussion of the golden rule BUILD YOUR SHARE DURING THE GROWTH STAGE OF THE MARKET – AND TAKE YOUR PROFIT DURING THE MATURE AND DECLINE STAGES (Chapter 9).]

The Size of the Opportunity

The size of the opportunity is one of the factors which should figure prominently in the operator's planning prior to his deciding whether or not he wishes to play. For instance, if he is a small manufacturer and the market he is proposing to move into promises to become a very big one he needs to be sure he has available the resources that will be necessary to maintain a leadership position.

It may well be possible for him to 'win' in the shorter term. He may be faster off the mark and first into the market with the new development. But if it is a big market and his competitors are big companies that are effectively managed, well equipped, financially strong, and the market is of consequence to them, then he must expect that they will 'strike back'.

In the 'strike back' they will use their superior resources to the full. The smaller operators competitive advantage will need to be strong enough to withstand this counter attack, in particular he will need to be sure that his own resources are sufficiently strong to ensure that he is not overwhelmed. If he does not have full confidence that his competitive advantage is strong enough or his resources adequate he may be well advised not to play.

For the big company a very big market potential is unlikely to be an outstanding problem. For the big operator the requirement is a very different one. He will need to be sure that the market he is considering, and in particular its potential, is large enough to warrant the attention of his resources. If he is to concentrate his effort (and this is normally an essential for success) he will need to limit the number of projects in which he engages. It is important that the projects chosen for action are worthy of the time and resources required. They must have the potential to produce a profit that not only shows a satisfactory level of percentage return but a satisfactory absolute level of profit.

■ *Here we are adding to the golden rule. Not only is it necessary to be sure you are going to win, you must also be sure that the prize for winning will be worth while to your business.*

This golden rule acts to concentrate management's thoughts on the importance of winning. The economic reasoning behind the rule is clearly centred on the fact that if you win in the market-place you should be able to turn your success into a higher level of profitability. The stronger your market leadership (i.e. the more you win) the higher should be your profit making ability.

All investment proposals should be compiled, and assessed, in a realistic manner. Those that promise to achieve a second or lower place in the market should receive particularly close attention. With the application of additional skill and resource can they be turned into 'winners'? – if not, they break the golden rule and require some very special reason for acceptance.

The business also needs to be sure it is concentrating its efforts to 'win' in the right markets. The opportunity cost to the big company of competing in a small market could be very high. The ultimate cost for the small company attempting to 'win' in a very large market could also be very high.

The effect of winning on the morale and attitude of personnel in the business is worthy of consideration. It is almost impossible to generate a high level of morale in a company that is losing. The management that is winning has a powerful 'tool' to help develop a strong and vibrant morale right through the business.

Chapter 7

The Pursuit is as Important as the Attack

*without a positive pursuit
the most successful attack can be dissipated*

Many of the golden rules of business strategy have been developed from military strategy. Carl von Clausewitz, the renowned military strategist, in his book *On War* (1832) states: "Under any conceivable circumstances the fact holds good, that without a pursuit no victory can have a great effect, and that, however short the career of victory may be, it must always lead beyond the first steps in pursuit."

In war the case for the pursuit would appear very obvious. The general who wins a particular battle cannot stand still; if he does, his enemies are likely to re-group and eventually counter-attack. If he fails to consolidate his victory it may be taken from him. A successful pursuit not only secures the victory, it ensures the enemy will not be allowed to re-group, and it provides the general with territorial and possibly many other benefits.

One of the often quoted and outstanding military examples of the importance of the pursuit is the campaign of Field Marshal Montgomery in North Africa during World War II. The decisive initial battle (i.e. the attack) was at Alamein late in 1942. There were other important battles, but the victory at Alamein was followed by a successful pursuit of Rommel's army across North Africa. Eventually the army was routed and the whole of North Africa fell to the allies.

Application of the 'Pursuit' in Business

The businessman is, to some considerable degree, in the same position as the general. If he makes a successful attack – for instance, the launch of a new brand into an established market – it will be vitally important that he 'follows up' (i.e. pursues) his attack. He will need to consolidate his brand launch.

The sampling promotion and the heavy launch advertising may have been successful in obtaining the first purchase by the consumer. But he must be sure to get the 'repeat' buy – this is all important if consumers are to develop the buying habit. After only one consumer purchase, the new brand will be vulnerable. Many consumers will be balanced in their approach – they may need the 'extra' incentive to make a repeat purchase. And if the repeat is lost they may not come back again. There will be a need for a strong follow-up promotion (i.e. the pursuit).

Competitors could have been taken by surprise by the initial launch of the new brand. However, if they are actively managed they are likely to strike back rapidly. It will be vital to obtain the important repeat sales before the strike-back enters the market.

When a new brand, or a re-launched established brand, enters a market it is invariably looking for sampling which in turn will lead to market share and ultimately to volume. The volume is of significance for it will allow investment in plant to be used economically and also provide for a lower level of unit cost. And a lower level of unit cost will be of great importance in winning the market place battles and ultimately providing a satisfactory level of profit contribution.

The 'pursuit' is very much concerned with ensuring the volume is held and developed into the future. The volume is contained in the repeat sales, and the 'pursuit' is all about ensuring the repeat sales are maximized.

■ *This is the economic backing for the 'pursuit' in business. It is required to reinforce the initial sampling. It is concerned to bring about the 'repeat buy', and from the repeaters come regular customers who make up the brand volume. Volume is the key factor in obtaining low production and distribution unit costs. The lower level unit costs*

*should mean a much higher brand contributory margin – and from
the margin come the funds necessary to develop and defend the brand,
and the brand's profit.*

The Importance of the Attack

This chapter is particularly concerned with the 'pursuit' as this is the
subject of the golden rule under discussion. The fact that the 'pursuit'
is as important – and in certain circumstances possibly more important – than the original attack, should not be allowed to obscure the
fact that a successful attack is of vital significance. Without a successful attack it may be questioned whether or not a pursuit is appropriate. With an unsuccessful attack some form of rescue operation may
well be necessary, but a rescue operation should not be confused with
a pursuit.

Failure to Carry out a Successful 'Pursuit'

The cost of not carrying out a successful pursuit can be extensive. It
could well mean the end of the particular venture.

If a pursuit is not carried out then the project will rest on the
results obtained in the initial attack. It is always possible that these
results could be sufficient to ensure a reasonable future for the project
– for instance, if a new brand has a performance advance which gives
it a significant competitive advantage, then this in itself could be
enough to bring back a satisfactory number of those sampled as repeat buyers. However, lack of a 'pursuit' could damage the new brand,
particularly in the three specific areas:

1. From competitive counter-attacks.
2. Inability to hold 'waiverers'.
3. Failure to exploit potential.

1. Competitive Counter-attacks

Worthwhile competitors would certainly not allow their market share to disappear without a struggle. They could be expected to counter-attack with a view to regaining any losses. Their attack may be of a tactical nature in the first instance, but this would probably be followed by a major operation featuring an appropriate product advancement and with considerable investment backing.

It is clearly vitally important that a successful 'pursuit' should have been mounted before the competitive major operation enters the market.

Without a successful 'pursuit' the competitive counter-attack is likely to be much more effective. The extent of this effectiveness must depend on the particular circumstances. However, at this stage of the new brand's life relatively small losses in market share can be very expensive when viewed over the longer term.

2. Inability to Hold 'Waiverers'

The new brand may prove particularly attractive to some consumers. Its purpose could be exactly in line with their requirements, and its performance/price balance attractive to them. But to others the new brand may have a 'luke warm' appeal. They may like it, but in certain respects they have doubts, and they may be tempted to return to their 'regular' brand next time they purchase.

This second group of consumers are the 'waiverers'. They need to be converted to regular users. They need to be encouraged to continue buying after the sample. If they can be persuaded to stay with the brand for a period then buying it may become a habit, and they could become that most valued of customers, the regular buyer. The attractions of their old brand could weaken with time.

The 'pursuit' has the task of holding the 'waiverers'. Without a 'pursuit' they will probably be lost – and once lost getting them back can be a very expensive business.

3. Failure to Exploit Potential

The attack may have been successful in sampling many consumers – but not all of those available. For a variety of reasons (e.g. heavily stocked with a competitive brand) many could have decided against buying at the time of the attack. But they are going to be in the market again sometime in the future.

The 'pursuit' aims to build on the base set by the attack – to pick up those who have delayed buying, to reinforce the brand's promise and bring in those who have been 'sitting on the fence'. In short, the pursuit should play an important part in ensuring the potential is exploited.

■ *Having invested heavily in its attack and achieved a satisfactory level of success the company that fails to follow with a well-planned and directed 'pursuit' may put at risk all the good achieved by the attack.*

The thought that 'you can always pick up the position later' is one that should be thoroughly questioned. Sometimes it may be possible but more often failure to carry out a satisfactory 'pursuit' will mean starting all over again at a later date. And starting again means incurring all the costs of the attack for a second time.

If the target is worth attacking then it is also worth pursuing. If it isn't worth pursuing then the value of the attack should be questioned. This is a very general rule and, as is usually so with a general rule, it is generally correct. It emphasizes the very basic point that the attacking company should always plan beyond its initial attacking operation. And its business plan for the particular project should always look beyond the initial revenues and expenditures.

From its experience the company should be clear what it is prepared to accept as a reasonable investment period for the project, and when it (the project) should be expected to begin to make a contribution to profits. The time period is likely to vary from case to case depending upon the particular circumstances.

The project financial plan should include all the expenditures necessary to bring it through to a satisfactory level of profit. The costs of the various 'pursuit' activities should be included in the plan. If the plan cannot produce a satisfactory level of profit it should not be accepted for action. Where the plan does produce a satisfactory level of profit this will normally begin to flow after the initial launch costs have been met (i.e. during and after a successful 'pursuit').

If the company has decided in advance that the project will not be worth pursuing then it must be able to build a position in the initial attack which will enable it to make a satisfactory level of profit contribution without 'pursuit' investment. If it cannot do this then the project should not be accepted for action.

For a project to be able to meet this requirement (i.e. an ability to make a satisfactory level of profit contribution without 'pursuit' investment) would be unusual for most businesses. There will be the exceptional cases though, such as in markets where projects are expected to have very short life-cycles. For instance, it could be possible for a popular music record to rely entirely on its initial launch attack as its life-cycle may be limited to a few weeks, or even a few days.

The 'Pursuit' must be Tailored for the Particular Occasion

Just as the attacking general must be sure that his army is equipped with the right weapons and other apparatus to facilitate the pursuit, so also must the businessman be sure he is properly prepared for his follow-up operation.

Heavy artillery may have been a key factor in the general's initial attack, but for the pursuit the requirement may be for light armoured vehicles able to travel swiftly. The businessman may open his attack with heavy sampling but his pursuit may be better served by strong theme advertising or a follow-up promotion which works on those consumers who have already been sampled.

Clearly the pursuit must be tailored for the particular occasion. As the pursuit must follow directly after the initial attack the time available to make shorter term adjustments is likely to be very limited. The main constituents of the 'pursuit' will probably need to be planned and produced in advance.

There will be a need to have clear guidance as to the results likely to be achieved by the initial attack. To be able to forecast with full confidence the exact results of the attack will probably be impossible. But guidance, and the clearer the better, will be most valuable.

Testing and research should prove most helpful. For instance, it should be possible from a well-conducted testing to know, with a reasonable degree of accuracy, how many homes per 100 will react favourably to a door-to-door sample. Similarly, tests of other forms of sampling promotion should provide guidance as to the level of conversion they are likely to provide.

When the businessman has a clear view as to what his initial attack is likely to produce, then he can begin to formulate his plans for the pursuit.

The level of investment in the pursuit will need to be varied depending on the need. The basis can be planned in line with the need as shown by the testing programme.

What if the actual results from the initial attack vary greatly from the forecast? This is always possible. There may be competitive moves which were not foreseen; abrupt changes in trade conditions could seriously affect the reception of the initial attack; in certain cases, climatic conditions could be of consequence – factors such as these could make a major difference. The attacker would be wise to build a sensible degree of flexibility into his pursuit plans.

The flexibility should attempt to cover both an 'under-' and an 'over-'achievement in the launch attack. The costs of attempting to recover an under-achievement are usually reasonably clear, the opportunity costs of not meeting the rise in demand that will follow an over-achievement by the attack are more difficult to cover, but they can be substantial.

The timing of the pursuit is bound to be of great significance. When the attack has been highly successful then the follow-up needs to be in action before the enemy has time to re-group or to mount a counter-attack. The initial attack should get the first purchase; the 'pursuit' should ensure the vitally important first repeat and then go on to encourage a regular purchasing habit.

Timing of the entry of the 'pursuit' into the stores, and thence to the consumer, will clearly be of great importance. If it is too late the competitors will have been given time to strike back. If it is too early it could confuse the initial attack. Getting it exactly right will be impossible because there will be no one time when all consumers are ready to purchase, or when all storekeepers are prepared to feature.

Given this position, it is clearly better to be too early rather than too late.

> ■ *The extent of the investment in the pursuit should be directly influenced by the 'job to be done' and the corporate profit position. The company attacking may need to face the fact that the pursuit could justify a level of investment higher than that made for the initial launch attack.*

New brand launches, and new major brand re-launches, are normally made or broken in their first year. It follows that during this period they need all the backing that is possible within the limits imposed by a sound financial plan.

The old adage "In a brand's first year it is better and cheaper to overspend rather than underspend" certainly has many supporters in business, and the 'pursuit' would normally come within the first year.

All Sections of the Business are Involved in the 'Pursuit': The Significance of Pricing

The pursuit is usually considered in terms of sales promotion and brand advertising. This is understandable as they are two powerful marketing tools which have particularly important parts to play in both the initial attack and the 'pursuit'. However, 'pursuit' should go beyond both sales promotion and advertising. Product development may be involved. A major change in formulation rapidly after launch would be unlikely, but any defects that were missed in the earlier testing can be (and should be) corrected, and if any worthwhile new developments become available they should also be considered for use.

Production will be very much involved in meeting the demand for product. It will be important that any unit cost reductions that become possible with the higher volumes should be realized. The economies foreseen by the 'experience curve' should be available, but they do not happen of their own accord. Costs have to be pushed down the experience curve by positive management action.

At least one major promotion is likely to be a key part of the 'pursuit' plan. The nature and form of each promotion included will depend on the particular circumstances which apply for the attacking brand. The need to reinforce the initial sampling and to consolidate the trade distribution are among the considerations which would normally require suitably designed promotions.

Brand advertising is also likely to be of great consequence. The needs to establish the brand, its promise, its ability to deliver its promise (preferably better than any other brand), and to establish the brand personality, are all factors that require repeated attention throughout the 'pursuit' period.

The salesforce has a prominent role in the pursuit. Normally the pursuit will centre around a major promotion (or series of promotions) and this will involve 'special offer' packs or financially supported promotional operations. It will be most important to use these special offers skilfully in both their direction (i.e. where the special pack is placed) and in the quantity placed. A key factor will be the negotiation of special feature with the major outlets. And, of course, the salesforce has the responsibility for distribution (i.e. the stocking of the brand by a satisfactory number of retailers and wholesalers), and this will be of vital importance – the aim must be high-level distribution for the attacking brand, and where the number of brands carried by any specific retailer is strictly limited then the attacking brand should be preferred to the one pursued.

Price is a particularly important weapon to be used in the pursuit. While price can have a significant role to play in the tactical marketplace battles, it is a strategic 'tool' and should be used with considerable care.

Frequently it will be advantageous to use promotions to take care of the shorter term requirements. Promotions have the effect of changing a brand's value for a short period of time, and because they are of a temporary nature the change can be at a higher level.

Price can have a very special part to play in certain 'pursuit' plans. The classic price move whereby a new brand enters a growing market, gains clear leadership, and then lowers its price to consolidate the leadership position and to restrict the funds available to competitors with which to counter-attack, is well known.

This is a very aggressive use of price. It requires special circumstances to operate satisfactorily, but when used skilfully it can be most effective. It can seal off a market and provide a dominant position through the growth stage of the market, leading into a highly profitable maturity.

Of course, it is possible that in specific circumstances the pursuit plan could contain proposals for a price increase. This would require very careful handling because the pursuit is very much concerned with consolidating gains and price increases, particularly large ones, would not normally be considered helpful to consolidation.

■ *It should be repeated: price is a strategic consideration; it needs to be treated with care. Short-term tactical moves are probably best handled through promotions. Nevertheless, it will be important for the attacker to avoid being 'out-priced' during the pursuit; to be 'out-priced' at this time, in a market where consumers are very price conscious, could undermine the whole pursuit operation. It could even undermine the success of the attack.*

The Limitations of the Pursuit

In these notes the important contribution a well-planned and executed 'pursuit' can play in ensuring that a successful attack becomes an equally successful total operation, and longer term profit contributor, has been emphasized. The golden rule is right, the pursuit is invariably as important as the attack. However, it is necessary to consider the limitations of the pursuit.

The 'pursuit' works best as a 'reinforcing' agent – that is, it acts to reinforce with the consumer the brand qualities that have already been introduced and developed in the attack. In particular the pursuit is concerned to encourage those who have been sampled in the attack to become regular buyers, and also to encourage those who have thought about sampling, but have delayed actually trying, to move forward and sample.

Unfortunately many managements misuse the 'pursuit'. They expect it to achieve objectives for which it is not suited. For instance, if you launch a new brand and immediately after the launch come to the conclusion that you have the wrong brand purpose, and in turn the wrong promise in your advertising, the pursuit is not the right time or place to correct this position.

Similarly, if you decide you need to make extensive changes to your brand formula immediately after the attack, the 'pursuit' is unlikely to be the right time or place to do it. If the formula change is an advance then it could be that it can be made to work effectively, but if the change is one that would be noticed and possibly rejected by consumers who have accepted the brand following the initial attack, then it should not be used in the 'pursuit'.

The pursuit is not the place to make a major price increase. It is not the time to introduce a new advertising promise (i.e. one that is markedly different from the one that has been used through the attack).

■ *In general terms, the 'pursuit' is not the best time or place to introduce any major brand changes. Minor changes could be acceptable, particularly if they are improvements. Major changes invariably carry a degree of risk, and the pursuit is not the best place to be taking unnecessary risk.*

The 'pursuit' can be used to correct certain operational weaknesses. If the brand has failed to get adequate store distribution during the attack then the 'pursuit' can be used to help in the correction of this position. The 'pursuit' can similarly help to correct consumer sampling problems. But it is most important that the 'pursuit' should be allowed to concentrate on its primary job, and that is reinforcing the attack. The correction of operational problems must not be allowed to interfere with this. Usually they can be taken care of by other less costly approaches.

■ *When this golden rule is considered the discussion invariably centres on whether or not the 'pursuit' is, in fact, as important as the 'attack'.*

Whether it is, or is not, is not really of consequence. Business success requires a successful attack followed by a successful pursuit. On some occasions the 'attack' will need an exceptional investment backing, but the 'pursuit' which follows it will require only a relatively low level of support. On other occasions the positions will be reversed, with a lower level investment behind the 'attack', and a particularly strong 'pursuit'.

The important consideration is that the investment backing and the total effort employed should be 'right' for the particular requirement.

The need for a successful 'attack' is rarely ever challenged. It is accepted, and a plan that did not provide for it would most certainly be criticized. The need for a successful 'pursuit' is not so widely accepted. Plans which do not provide for it are often accepted for action.

The message of this golden rule is very clear. The 'pursuit' is vitally important, you must include it in your plans. Any plan that does not provide for it should be very closely questioned.

Chapter 8

Never Start a Price War Unless You're Sure You are Going to Win

price war winners are rare; losers are plentiful,
and losing can be both painful and costly

When the brands competing in a market engage in frequent price cutting, and this continues for a lengthy period, then it will be said that a 'price war' is in operation. A 'price war' is a sustained period of price cutting.

Price wars can be started deliberately or by accident. Those started by accident are the most frequent. A salesman reports a rumour picked up from one of his buyers that a particular competitor is moving prices down. Another salesman reports a similar rumour, and then an advertising executive remarks that space has been booked to make a special announcement. Rumour quickly makes this into a price move. The rumours are so strong that action is taken to get ahead of the competitor with the price reduction. The move prompts a counter move and so the spiral is in motion.

The rumours were, of course, incorrect. The competitor had no intention of reducing price; but this only becomes clear some months later. Everyone in the market has suffered, brand market shares have not really changed, and the whole exercise has been costly and unnecessary.

The cynics claim that by far the majority of 'accidental' price wars are caused by astute buyers, and by salesmen who have failed to book an order.

Fortunately accidental price wars can usually be controlled before they have caused extensive damage.

■ *Within a competitive business it is necessary to have a rumour collecting procedure. A rumour can be the precursor to the firm announcement of a competitive action. But rumours should always be checked and verified before they are accepted as the basis for action. The cynics have a point – buyers can have a vested interest in starting price action, and unsuccessful salesmen do tend to look for excuses.*

This golden rule is concerned with price wars that are started deliberately. An operator within the market has decided that a price war is the most suitable form of action available to him to achieve a particular business objective; he therefore moves forward and starts a price war.

Why Should this Golden Rule be Followed?

The record shows very clearly that if you enter a price war and lose, then the whole exercise is likely to be very costly to you. At the extreme, the cost could cause you to lose control of your business.

The development of the price war could mean that you will be forced to sell at prices which do not provide sufficient revenue to cover the costs of operating the business. While you may be able to live with this for a period, it is not a position that can be allowed to continue over the longer term.

The price war may be fought with one particular brand but its influence is likely to spread beyond this. Competitors may react in other markets and ultimately the whole business could be involved.

The price war may represent a fight of life or death for some of the competitors. When the stakes are as high as this sometimes the moves made are extreme and their consequences drastic.

The majority of price wars appear to end in a 'no-win' position. The aggressor fails to achieve his objectives, and the brands under attack suffer badly but still manage a recovery, possibly a limited one. It costs everyone concerned a considerable amount in terms of revenue foregone, and the 'wear and tear' on each contestant is invariably extensive.

Often even the winner finds his business 'exhausted' after the battle, and the task of returning prices to a more normal level is not always a simple exercise. Having become adjusted to the lower price levels customers may react adversely to the move upwards.

■ *All this argues very strongly that the golden rule should state "Never start a price war" and stop there. And many businessmen, probably a large majority, would agree with this.*

But the golden rule does not stop, it adds the phrase "unless you're sure you are going to win". This is of real significance and requires further discussion.

Can You Ever be Sure of Winning a Price War?

The simple and straightforward answer to this question must be "No". But again we have a golden rule which is using simplicity to help gain recognition.

The results which will flow from any move in business can never be forecast with complete accuracy. There will always be a degree of risk involved, even if in some instances the risk is very small.

If we instance a very major operation such as a new brand launch, it is certainly not possible to predict with complete accuracy just how the new brand will perform when it enters a real live national market operation. However, with careful preparation and detailed research and testing, it should be possible to make a reasonably accurate forecast.

Similar remarks apply to a price war. While a completely accurate forecast of results will not be possible (you cannot be sure of winning) it should be possible to make a reasonably accurate forecast of developments within the market as the price war develops.

■ *What the golden rule is saying is "Take great care before you start a price war. Research all the aspects, check and re-check the figures in your forecasts, use both a 'belt and braces'; only if you can forecast an overwhelming victory should you go ahead. This is not an area for taking chances." But this is a rather long statement to be memorized in a golden rule.*

You Can Win a Price War – And it Can be Very Profitable

The dangers and the risks of starting a price war have been stated in the paragraphs above. But, of course, it is possible to win a price war, and the prize for winning can be very substantial.

What do we mean by winning? The answer must be to achieve your chosen objective at what is considered to be a satisfactory cost. In practice, price wars are invariably concerned with gaining market share (and sales volume) from a competitor or series of competitors. Normally the aggressor is intent on improving his own position and greatly weakening the position of his competitors.

The classic example of a successful price war operation often quoted is that of a market where there is one major operator who holds a substantial share of the market (say 50%), and the remainder of the market is held by a large number of small operators, none of whom holds more than a 5% share.

With his great volume lead the major operator should have a very substantial advantage in unit cost (for the same product) over all the other competitors. He is able to reduce his unit selling price and put great pressure on all the other competitors in the market. All of them will feel this and some will be forced out of business.

After a period of the pressure the major operator may have increased his market share to say 70% and reduced the number of competitors markedly. Those that remain will be experiencing a very difficult time.

The major operator should not have suffered extensively during this period. His unit margin will have been reduced (due to the price cut) but his volume will have increased, and so his total margin should not have changed substantially.

The major operator is then able to bring the price war to an end. He will have increased his market share from 50% to 70% (i.e. an increase of 40% for him). Given that the total volume of the market has remained unchanged he will also have increased his volume by 40%. Of course, it is always possible that the price reductions will also have brought about an increase in the total market.

Now the major operator can, if he wishes, set about bringing unit prices back up. The competitors remaining in the market are unlikely to object, indeed they will probably be desperately keen to follow the leader's move.

And so, after the price war, the major operator will have increased his volume by 40% at a relatively small cost (or possibly no cost at all). He will have the additional gross margin the 40% extra volume contributes. And beyond this the additional volume should have provided a reduction in unit cost for all his production. Not a bad return for a relatively inexpensive operation! And into the future he will be a dominant leader; his competitors will appreciate that he is 'not to be annoyed'.

■ *Of course, it can be argued that this classic example is far too simple and easy for the real world. This is probably so but, nevertheless, it does act to show that aggressive pricing can be made to work and the returns it is capable of bringing can be spectacular.*

Planning the Price War

On many occasions it would seem that a price war has been entered into as an emotional reaction. The chief executive of Company A has had his plans for the introduction of a new performance advance in one of his brands thwarted on a number of occasions by the price activity of his competitors, B, C and D. The chief executive has had enough, he is determined that his competitors should be 'taught a lesson' and so he starts a price war.

Price wars started this way are rarely a success. They usually come to an indeterminate end without a winner and with many losers. Indeed, the final phase is usually about 'face-saving'.

Successful price activities are invariably planned with great care.

They require skilled research, thorough preparation, decisive action, adept timing, and probably a little good fortune. If a price war should 'go wrong' it can be very difficult to get it back under control. The down-side risk can be high, sometimes very high. At the extreme, the whole business can be at risk. Careful preparation is most certainly essential.

The first requirement is that the business concerned should be convinced that a price war is the best way to achieve the particular objective. This means that the business should have carried out a detailed review of all the practical means available to it and have decided that 'price' is the weapon that is best suited to achieve the objective.

The planning for a price war operation should receive the same form of detailed preparation as any major business operation which requires a substantial investment and a high level of management resource. With price war planning certain considerations need specific attention. The following are of particular significance:

- *What is the extent of the resources available to fight the war?*
  This question applies both to the aggressor and to others likely to be involved in the war.

  Price wars can be expensive. It is important to know what resources you have, and have available to you, to wage the war. Equally it is most important to be as sure as possible of the level of resources available to your competitor.

  There will be many operating skills which, if you possess them at a higher level than your competitors, will help you to fight the war successfully. But in the final analysis, the level of resources available to you and to your competitors is likely to be of vital importance.

  Within the total resources available, cash is sure to have a particular importance. A shortage of cash during a critical period of the war could prove decisive.

- *Competitors – their ownership, their management, and their operating ability.*
  Competitors should feature in considerable detail in the review of resources. And beyond this their brands, their strengths and weaknesses, should have been covered in full

in the marketing study that is clearly an essential part of any price war preparation. However, here we are concerned with a series of factors which can be difficult to assess with any high degree of accuracy, but which can be of very great significance in determining the result of a price war.

A competitive business can be owned by a multi-national operator, a conglomerate, an independent company with a local stock market listing, or be under the private ownership of a family. The form of ownership, and beyond this the character and outlook of the people concerned, can be all important in the way the price war is conducted.

If the competitor is part of a major, well-financed multi-national, and the market concerned is of importance to this owner, then the battle is unlikely to be a short and easy one. The local managers will probably be under instructions to limit expenditure but to 'stay with your position'. With this type of competitor the aggressor should certainly have considered very carefully if a price war is the best way to reach his objective.

Should the competitor be an independent company quoted on the local stock exchange then his share price will be of very considerable consequence to him. If it drops rapidly then his independence could be threatened. Of course, there is always the possibility that any new owner could be a much more substantial operator and better equipped to fight the war.

If the competitor is an independent family firm then the attitude and approach of the senior members is likely to be critical. Some families would fight to the death before giving in, others would be keen to sell out at the first sign of action.

Whatever the ownership, the character and ability of the people actually managing the competitive business is sure to be of major consequence. Price wars can become very personal. They can be very frustrating and at times emotional. Patience can often be an important requirement if they are to be pursued successfully.

The need is to know of the training, character, and track

record of the managers engaged in making the key decisions within the competitive businesses; to know how they are likely to react to intense pressure, and be prepared to use this knowledge in the war.

- *Vulnerability.*
You may be in a strong, almost impregnable, position in the market in which you propose to wage the price war, but are you vulnerable in another market? And could one of your competitors make this vulnerability work against you?

   It is not uncommon for a business to maintain a brand in a market where it is not a serious competitor merely as a form of 'counter-offensive weapon' against a possible price attack in a market where it derives a major part of its profit.

   "Check your possible vulnerability before you go to war" must be the maxim. And remember that your selected victim may be prepared to seek help from others who have an ability to hurt you.

- *Your ability to raise prices after the war.*
It is probable that your ability to earn the level of profit you expect after the price war will require you to return selling prices to a more 'normal' level. Are you sure this will be possible?

   Again you can never be absolutely sure but you need to have a very clear view that the necessary uplift will be possible and that it will not mean a fall in volume. In practice, if the price cuts during the war have been very deep it will often be necessary to bring them back up gradually. A lengthy period of time may be necessary and it is important that full allowance should be made for this in the financial plans.

- *The movement of the market.*
It would be reasonable to expect that during the price war the volume of the total market will increase markedly. Much will depend on the development of the market prior to the commencement of the war, and to the degree of elasticity in demand for the products concerned.

   If the market is already fully developed then it could be that the price will mean only a small change in the size of the total market.

The movement of the market can clearly have a major effect on the revenue the various competing operators can expect to receive from it during the price war. It will be important to get the estimate 'right' in the financial planning.

- *Other promotional investments.*

During the course of a price war there will be a temptation to restrict the investment in other promotional investments, such as advertising and sales merchandising. It will be reasoned that the price cut in itself is expensive enough. This could be an unwise decision.

Much will depend on the particular market and on the trading conditions which apply within it. If the regular customer picks up a pack of the brand and then discovers when he reaches the check-out that he is lucky as the brand is selling at a special low price, then the manufacturer has achieved very little. However, if the price reduction is given suitable publicity then the regular customer may be tempted to buy more than one pack, the infrequent buyer may be tempted into the market, and those who usually buy competitive brands may be tempted to change.

It can be argued that good brand theme advertising is of even greater significance during a price war. With many brands it will be important to maintain a quality image. Extreme price cutting could cause an impression of 'cheapness' and good brand theme advertising can help to offset this.

This whole topic will require careful consideration when the financial plans for the price operation are drawn up.

- *Sales and marketing effectiveness.*

Earlier we have referred to the importance of overall effectiveness in managing the business for an operator caught up in a price war. Now we are referring to a specific part of the business operation – sales and marketing.

How you operate in the market-place during a price war can be of great significance to the outcome of the war. Of course, the basic efficiency in operation throughout the business is fundamental, but sales and marketing effectiveness beyond this is special.

The timing and the selection of the various moves will have a particular importance. In consumer markets, you will have to decide if, when, and where, to use promotions other than price. Should 'extra-weight' packs be employed? Is there a place for coupons? When handling the trade, should 'throughput bonuses' or in-store merchandising activities be employed? The brand may have a number of pack sizes – should they all be used at the one time, or could greater effect be obtained by the use of a single size only? Could the various trade channels (e.g. independents, multiples, co-operatives), be used in special operations? Should the various offers be advertised? For industrial and service markets, similar manoeuvres are available.

These are just a few of the pertinent questions that need to be asked and answered. Skill in handling such operations can have a material effect on the outcome of the price war. They can be of particular importance in determining for just how long the war drags on. A skilled operator can use 'delaying' tactics which could prove particularly costly to an aggressor.

It must also be accepted that 'bluff' and 'counter bluff' frequently feature prominently within the action of the war. The skilled and experienced operator is more likely to be able to handle these situations successfully than is the 'amateur'.

- *Be sure of the 'prize'.*
From these notes it must be clear that a price war is most certainly not free of risk. Indeed, without careful assessment and planning the risk can be extensive.

In these circumstances it is worth making a very careful check on the value of the 'prize' for winning the war. This calculation is an important part of the original proposal for the price war project. The suggestion here is that it is so important to be as sure as is possible just how much a 'win' will bring that a detailed check would be very worth while and should be made from time to time as the war progresses.

Once you have started on a price war, pulling back becomes

extremely difficult. Certain of your competitors may sense victory and so will be unlikely to allow you to escape without making full payment.

Loss of face should certainly not get in the way of a withdrawal if such a move makes good business sense – but the probability is that it will!

All this says that before you enter you must be very sure that the war is worth fighting, and worth winning.

If a company is considering the launch of a major new brand into one of its biggest markets it will, if it is sensible, give the project top priority in both planning and operation. It will ensure that fully competent personnel work on the project with access to the highest levels in the company. And it will ensure that the 'key' decisions concerning the project are taken by the Chief Executive. This is all very reasonable and to be expected in a well-managed business.

■ *The planning and operation of a price war deserves, and should get, the same level of resource and senior management attention. And the Chief Executive should take responsibility for the 'key' decisions.*

The launch of a major new brand is a big operation, and success can be very important to the business. But if the launch is unsuccessful, the company is likely to continue in business and possibly recover the position later.

A company which loses a long and expensive price war is unlikely to find recovery a simple proposition. A price war operation most certainly deserves the very best planning and execution the business can give it.

NEVER START A PRICE WAR UNLESS YOU ARE SURE YOU ARE GOING TO WIN.

Successful Price War in the U.S. Cigarette Market

The U.S. tobacco market must rate as one of the biggest consumer product markets in the country. In 1992 it was estimated to have a revenue value of over $45bn.

During April 1993 one of the competitors within the market made a very aggressive price move – a move which was hailed as the beginning of an industry price war.

Within the market the two leading competitors were Philip Morris and R.J. Reynolds. Philip Morris was considered to be very strong financially. The company had used its high level of earnings from tobacco to fund an extensive development in the food industry (among other companies it owned both General Foods and Kraft – two of the largest food businesses in the U.S.). However, it is important to note that despite the size of the food business, tobacco was thought to contribute approximately two-thirds of the Philip Morris total profit.

During 1988 R.J.R. Nabisco, the owner of R.J. Reynolds, had been the subject of one of the largest and most spectacular corporate takeovers in U.S. history. As a result of the takeover the company carried a very high level of debt.

The 'smaller' companies in the market were nevertheless companies of considerable size. American Tobacco Company (a subsidiary of American Brands) was estimated to have a U.S. tobacco revenue of some $1.8bn in 1992. Both Brown and Williamson (a major subsidiary of B.A.T.) and the Ligget Group were also substantial companies.

The U.S. cigarette market had been in decline for a number of years. During 1992 the decline rate was estimated at approximately 2.5%.

In 1992 the leading company in the market was Philip Morris with a share of some 42%. Within this total share the company's leading brand, and dominant market leader, *Marlboro,* held 21–22%. The *Marlboro* brand market share was some three times the level of the second brand *Winston,* owned by R.J. Reynolds. However, the *Marlboro* brand had been losing market share through recent periods. In 1989 it had approximately 26% of the market, but by early 1993 this had been reduced to 21%.

The most dramatic development in the market over the five years between 1987 and 1992 had been the introduction and development of a series of 'discount' brands (brands priced at as much as 45% below the leading brands). In 1982 this type of brand was virtually non-existent. By 1990 they accounted for 20% of the market, and by 1992 they were reported to have moved to a share in excess of 35%.

It is important to appreciate that these 'discount' brands were manufactured and marketed by the operators who competed in the premium sector of the market. All of the major companies had discount brands and in some cases marketed them aggressively. For some of the companies their discount brands had become the major part of their business.

In early April 1993 Philip Morris made a price adjustment to allow for a cut of 40 cents per pack in the suggested retail price of *Marlboro*. (In fact, retail prices were cut by 40 to 70 cents per pack.) Philip Morris also mounted a major sales promotion in support of *Marlboro*. A cut of 40 cents per pack retail meant a reduction from $2.10 to $1.70 (i.e. a cut in price of approximately 20%).

R.J. Reynolds and the other manufacturers of premium brands were forced to follow the *Marlboro* lead and to make price cuts.

In July 1993 Philip Morris announced that the price cut it had previously presented as temporary was to be permanent and extended to the rest of its premium brands. The company also announced price adjustments which appeared to be aimed at converting the price structure in the market from a three stage to a two stage position. In addition Philip Morris began to give much more support to its own discount brand *Basic*. The brand was backed by an advertising campaign and extra merchandising support.

By March 1994 Philip Morris was quoted as claiming a total company share of 46% of the U.S. cigarette market (i.e. a gain of 4 points over the 42% share in 1992). The *Marlboro* brand alone had grown from a share of 22% to 27% i.e. a gain of 5 points, and the Philip Morris discount brand *Basic* had risen to become the No. 3 brand in the total market.

On Wall Street at the time of the *Marlboro* price cut Philip Morris stock dropped from $64 to $49. However, by March 1994 it had recovered to $54 (i.e. $10 below the pre-price cut level).

Most of the financial reporters and other business writers commenting on this case have talked in terms of Philip Morris starting a price war in April 1993. However, it can be argued that the price war was actually started between the period 1987 and 1992 by the smaller companies with the aggressive promotion of their 'discount' brands.

If the smaller competitors did start the price war then they certainly moved against the golden rule NEVER START A PRICE WAR UNLESS

YOU'RE SURE YOU ARE GOING TO WIN. There would seem to be no reason why they should believe they could possibly win a price war against a competitor such as Philip Morris.

Philip Morris was a dominant market leader. The total volume of the company's brands was at least twice the level of its nearest competitor. The Philip Morris record in the U.S. tobacco market was one of outstanding success. The management was both effective and efficient. In all probability the company's unit cost of both manufacture and distribution was the lowest of all the competitors in the market. In general the company's brands were in very good shape.

The Philip Morris Company's financial strength was very evident. Of all the competitors it was the best positioned financially to fight and win a price war.

If you start a price war against a competitor as well positioned as this, you are most certainly moving against the golden rule. You cannot expect to win, indeed you are almost sure to lose.

The position reached in March 1994 indicated that the smaller companies (and this included R. J. Reynolds) were facing difficulties. Their revenue from their premium brands would have fallen drastically as the result of the price reduction. Their revenue from their 'discount' brands would, in all probability, also have fallen. Their prospects of making market share and volume gains into the future were greatly diminished. The market leader had made it very clear to his competitors that he would 'stand no nonsense' – they must appreciate their position, or get badly hurt.

If we accept that Philip Morris did start the price war in April 1993, can we be sure that the company did so in accord with the golden rule?

The answer to this question must be "Yes". Philip Morris had very good reason to believe it could win a price war. The company would be aware of its own and competitors' cost structures and brand strengths. It would also have known of its own strong financial position and the problems of its competitors.

It was known that Philip Morris had been engaged in a programme of price testing for its *Marlboro* brand in the periods before the price cut. From these tests the company should have gained clear guidance of the probable effect on sales volume of varying levels of price reduction.

The three key questions that were facing the Philip Morris management were:

(i) "How big an investment do we need to make to get our market share back to a satisfactory level?"
(ii) "Can we get a satisfactory return from that investment, and in what time period?"
(iii) A question which is of great importance: "What will be our position into the future if we do not take action?"

In a statement made at the time of the April 1993 price cut the company stated "Philip Morris U.S.A. . . . announced a major shift in business strategy designed to increase market share and grow long-term profitability in a highly price sensitive market environment". It would seem that the Philip Morris management had asked and answered the questions to their satisfaction.

The price move by Philip Morris in April 1993 has been debated at great length by economists, business managers, financial journalists, and many others with a profound interest in business affairs. Opinions on the move vary from the extremes of "Philip Morris have made a brilliant move" to "the move will prove a disaster". In March 1994, one year after the action, the jury was still out. More time and experience was needed before a worthwhile judgement could be made. But opinion appeared to be moving to the view that Philip Morris would win the price war and over the longer term their move would be seen as a successful one.

In January 1995 Philip Morris reported on its domestic U.S. tobacco business. Its full year 1994 operating revenues reached $11.1bn, up 8.6% from 1993, and operating income advanced by 17.6% to $3.3bn. The gains were driven largely by continued growth in *Marlboro* volume, and this reflected the success of the company's pricing strategy, as well as effective marketing and sales programmes.

Philip Morris also reported that domestic shipment volume for the year was 219.4 billion units, a gain of 12.7%, compared to a 6.2% increase for the entire U.S. cigarette industry. Shipments of *Marlboro* in the U.S. rose 27%, to 137.7 billion units. The volume gains gave Philip Morris a record shipment share of 44.8%, an increase of 2.6 share points from 1993, while *Marlboro's* shipment share rose 4.6 points, to 28.1%.

The company claimed that at the retail level, it had established a new share record for its flagship brand, *Marlboro*. Data from Nielsen North America show that *Marlboro* captured a record 29.4% of the U.S. retail market in the fourth quarter, an increase of 7.4 share points compared with March 1993 before Philip Morris announced its *Marlboro* pricing strategy. The Nielsen figures also show that the company's overall share in the fourth quarter reached 46.4%, a gain of 4.7 share points from March 1993.

Following this Philip Morris report the jury would appear to be well equipped to reach a verdict in this classic case of price-war activity.

If the smaller companies in the U.S. domestic tobacco market did start the price war with their discount brand activity they will now be aware that breaking the golden rule NEVER START A PRICE WAR UNLESS YOU'RE SURE YOU ARE GOING TO WIN can be a very costly and painful business.

If the price war was started by Philip Morris then it would seem that they have demonstrated very clearly that if you are sure you are going to win (and in this case they had good reason to feel very confident that they would win), you can make a price war a very effective and beneficial operation.

Effectiveness and Efficiency in Operation

In all business engagements, whether they be straightforward brand battles for market share or a price war, the business that is effective and efficient in its operations will be that much better placed than one that is in some way inefficient.

■ *For a competitor who is intent on winning a price war the need for a high level of effectiveness and efficiency in operation is paramount. An important adjunct to the golden rule* NEVER START A PRICE WAR UNLESS YOU'RE SURE YOU WILL WIN *is that before you start the war you should "be sure you have at least a competitive advantage, and preferably a significant one, in product cost".*

Of course, a price war can be won without an advantage in product cost. As we have already considered, the reserves available to the contestants in the war could overcome a cost differential. But this would be a very costly way of fighting the war, and it is clearly preferable for an aggressor to go into the war knowing that he has a unit cost advantage over his competitors.

To be sure of a unit cost advantage, possibly a significant one, the aggressor will need:

1. Volume.
2. Effectiveness and efficiency in operation.

Volume is normally one of the most important factors in obtaining low-level unit costs. It makes possible the economic use of highly automated production facilities and other large-scale and effective operating plant. Distribution costs can also be very acutely affected by volume, particularly if the distributors' margin is included within the costs.

If you have effectiveness and efficiency in operation then you should be able to make full and effective use of your volume. And if you are in an industry where volume does not play an important part in your costs, the requirement that you be effective and efficient is even more important for it becomes the one factor that will enable you to be the low-cost producer and to have a cost advantage.

It may be possible to get a competitive advantage in unit cost without a volume advantage (i.e. by effectiveness and efficiency alone) but usually it is very difficult. To get a significant competitive advantage in unit costs (the kind of advantage an aggressor in a price war would like to have) it would normally be necessary to have a worthwhile volume advantage *and* to be effective and efficient. To have the volume advantage without the appropriate efficiency could result in a competitive disadvantage – not a desirable position for an aggressor (or any competitor) who wants to win a price war.

■ *The message is clear – Be effective and efficient in your operations, and be sure you keep improving.*

A Low-Margin Policy: Aggressive Pricing

Company A is a well financed business competing in a market which is currently in its early growth stage. A is the market leader with a share of approximately 30% of the market. A has a number of competitors the largest of which has a market share of approximately 20%. The market is believed to have an outstanding potential. A is a well-managed company, it has a modern, effectively equipped plant, it has vacant production facilities, and it operates very efficiently. The competitors vary in size and standing – many are smaller companies with limited resources.

Company A takes a decision to follow a low-margin policy with its brand in the market. A has, in effect, decided that all competitors in the market should work with low unit margins, and with low unit profitability.

The approach followed by Company A in this example is not an unusual one for a company operating in a growth market which has considerable potential, and where the competitive position is similar to the one outlined. It is certainly an example of the use of price in an aggressive manner, but it would not normally be considered as the opening of a price war.

In a price war there is usually a spiralling of prices downward, each competitor cutting under the others in the fight for business. The low-margin approach involves the setting of what some competitors may view as an inadequately low level of margin but it does not provide for a spiralling down.

The low-margin approach is likely to be a longer term strategic move. It acts to limit the ability of competitors to compete, and in particular the lower level returns are intended to discourage any potential new competitor from making the necessary investments for entry.

While the low-margin approach tends to be viewed differently from a price war, to some extent the results it is likely to achieve are very similar. Under both approaches small and inefficient competitors will probably be forced out of business. There may be a difference in the timing as the low-margin method tends to be longer term in its effect, but ultimately it will probably act to reduce the number of competitors. Both approaches are usually aimed at bringing into being a dominant market leader.

■ *The same basic golden rule applies for the low-margin approach as for a price war. Before you move along the low-margin track you need to be very sure your will 'win'. To take the low-margin approach and to 'fail' could prove very expensive.*

Low Unit Margin Policy: Price War

Persil Automatic is possibly the most successful brand introduced into the U.K. grocery markets since 1945. The brand was launched into the U.K. national low suds washing powder market in 1969. At this time the market was relatively small but it clearly had the potential to grow and to capture over 90% of the total U.K. washing powder market.

In 1969 most of the washing machines in use in the U.K. were known as 'twin tubs'. In this type of machine it is normal to use what is known as a 'high suds' washing powder. *Persil* soap powder was 'high suds' and was the market leader. During this period, a new type of machine known as an 'automatic' was beginning to move into the U.K. washing machine market.

The 'automatic' had a number of advantages over the 'twin tub' and there was little doubt that it would ultimately become the predominant washing machine in U.K. households. However, there was some debate as to how long the conversion would take. The 'automatic' machines required a 'low suds' washing powder. *Persil Automatic* was a 'low suds' powder specially formulated for the new machines.

Persil Automatic quickly established itself as the leader of the U.K. 'low suds' washing powder market. By 1974 the market had grown substantially and was expected to continue growing through the next 10 to 15 years.

At this time a strategic pricing decision was taken on *Persil Automatic*. Henceforth the brand was to run with a relatively low unit margin. Brand profit development was to come from volume.

The pricing decision was intended to encourage the rapid development of the market, restrict the funds available to competitive brands to attack *Persil Automatic,* 'and ensure that it was difficult for the distributor brands to market a powder with a reasonable level of performance at a price which was significantly below that of *Persil Automatic.*

In 1973 Procter and Gamble launched *Bold Automatic,* a 'low suds' powder, and gave it extensive advertising and promotional support. In 1979 P&G launched *Daz Automatic* and Lever launched *Surf Automatic* – both brands were strongly supported. In 1981 P&G launched *Ariel Automatic,* which also received extensive advertising and promotional support. In 1982 P&G launched a re-staged *Bold Automatic* with a fabric softener contained within the product. Throughout the 1970s and 1980s, the retail multiple chains were very active with distributor brands in the 'low suds' market.

Despite all this activity *Persil Automatic* held over 40% of the U.K. low suds market in 1983. The brand was a dominant market leader, outselling any competitive brand by some 2 to 1. Distributor brands held less than 10% of the market.

Many factors contributed to the *Persil Automatic* success. The low-margin policy followed by the brand through this period was clearly an important consideration. Lever certainly did not believe it was involved in a price war – there was no spiralling down of prices. Competitors in the market did not talk publicly of being involved in a price war but, of course, they would probably have preferred *Persil Automatic* to have followed a higher margin policy.

Estimating the Cost of a Price War

Before starting a price war the aggressor needs to have a clear idea as to how much waging the war is likely to cost him. Only if he knows how much cost is involved can he begin to consider whether or not the whole operation will be worth while. A simple formula which provides a very broad indication of the cost of a price war to a particular company would be:

$$(MC^1 \times SV^1) - (MC^2 \times SV^2) = \text{Cost of Price War}$$

where:

MC^1 = Marginal contribution per unit without the price war (£).

SV^1 = Sales volume estimate, without the price war, through the price war period.

MC^2 = Marginal contribution per unit with the price war (£).

SV^2 = Sales volume estimate, with the price war, through the price war period.

This is a simple enough formula, but, of course, its value depends on the accuracy of the figures contained within it.

Practical businessmen will quickly state that it is impossible to calculate accurately the 'Marginal contribution per unit', and they are correct. But good accountants should be able to make a creditable stab at the calculation and provide figures that are 'reasonable working estimates'.

Worthwhile estimates of the marginal contribution will be difficult; worthwhile estimates of the sales volume will be even more so. No doubt detailed analysis of sales volume movements through any previous periods of price activity will be helpful. The computer, with its ability to analyse and prepare forecasts, should also be invaluable. But during price wars, emotion often comes to the fore, and sales levels can take exceptional moves. And, of course, it will be necessary to estimate the time period of the war – not an estimate that can be made with great confidence of it being 'right'.

Worthwhile estimates, that have any real probability of being accurate, will be extremely difficult to prepare across this whole spectrum. This is clearly an area where sound judgement will be of the highest value. It is quite possible to wage a successful price war and increase profits in the process; it is also possible to wage a successful price war and find that it has a horrific effect on profits.

It is essential that a realistic estimate of the cost of waging the price war should be available to the operator before he takes the decision to 'go to war'.

■ *It is accepted that preparing such an estimate is extremely difficult. Sound judgement will be at a very high premium. But the fact that the task is a difficult one does not provide an acceptable excuse for not making the best possible effort to meet it. To enter a price war on a wave of emotion and/or because it appears 'easy' could prove to be a very costly, even fatal, decision.*

The Victim of a Price War

Many of the companies that become involved in price wars are not there by choice. They would prefer not to be involved. But if one of your competitors starts to use price aggressively and you see your brand market share beginning to slide, then if you want to retain your business you have no alternative – you have to become involved.

If you are the victim of a price war attack how should you react? It depends very much on your particular circumstances. The general aim must be to fight in such a way that you hold your market share and limit your expenditures while your competitors are forced to spend heavily and make no gain. The need is to ensure that you use your resources where you are likely to have an advantage; that you fight, as far as possible, on your home ground and that you retain the initiative through the course of the battle.

If you are the small man in the battle then you use those advantages that your size affords you. Flexibility is one such advantage that should be yours. You can use special packs prepared at short notice. If you employ differential pricing then you use this with *key* accounts and work to ensure you get all the help and assistance normally accorded to the small man.

If you are the big man then you employ the economy of scale which is yours and should provide you with lower unit costs for standard product. You avoid being thrown off your main line of attack, and you take care to be sensibly patient. You know that you are in a position to give the consumer best value over the medium term and so you play the game accordingly. You have greater resources and time should be on your side.

■ *Two basic points are of significance under this heading. If you are the small man and your business intelligence tells you that you are likely to be the subject of a price attack then you could be well advised to consider selling your business or merging it with a strong partner.*

You are likely to get a much better price and your brands have a better chance of survival if you do this before the attack rather than after.

Secondly, in price wars, as in all business battles of this kind, the business that is effective and efficient in its operations is much more likely to survive and prosper than is one that is ineffective. Be sure your business is in good shape before the battle starts, it may be too late to change after the battle.

Price is one of the most significant of strategic 'tools'. This is the basic message of the golden rule. Use it with great care.

The decision to start a price war is a strategic decision. It should have the same level of attention from senior management as any other major strategic proposal.

Before you start a price war you should be as confident as is possible that you have the resources and the ability to win. If you do not have this very high level of confidence, then don't start a war.

If you are ever in danger of losing a price war then don't let pride or stubbornness get in the way of an acceptable settlement.

The 'prize' if you win a major price war can be substantial – if you lose, or have to settle for a draw, the cost can be crippling. The golden rule is right: NEVER START A PRICE WAR UNLESS YOU'RE SURE YOU ARE GOING TO WIN.

Chapter 9

Build Your Brand Share During the Growth Stage of the Market

and take your profit during the mature and decline stages

Before discussing this particular golden rule it is necessary to consider the 'Three Stage' theory of market development. This theory argues that all markets pass through three stages:

1. Growth.
2. Maturity.
3. Decline.

During the growth stage the total market is growing. It is growing in terms of quantity consumption, and also in terms of value. During the mature stage the total volume, and value, of the market remains static. There may be some limited movements, both up and down, but they are not likely to be of great consequence. When a market goes into the decline stage the total volume, and value, falls.

It is important to appreciate that the theory does not attempt to prescribe the duration of the stages. It accepts that the periods will vary in length from market to market. It further accepts that the rates of growth and decline will also differ depending on the circumstances which apply in the particular markets.

As we shall see later, there is a considerable skill involved in forecasting accurately both the length of a particular market stage, and also its rate of rise or decline.

There are many other theories of market development. Most of them tend to be much more complex and have more than three stages. However, as a simple and basic approach the 'Three Stage' theory does appear to receive wide acceptance within the business world.

Defining the Market

If this golden rule is to have a practical application, there is a need to be clear just which market is under consideration. Beyond this there is a requirement for a geographical definition. For instance, are we considering the total toilet soap market, or the deodorant sector within the total market. And is our market that for the U.K., or is it for the whole of Europe, or for the whole world?

The importance of this need for a definition should be clear. Frequently a total market will have moved beyond its growth stage into maturity and possibly decline, but within it a particular sector may be enjoying strong growth.

Over time, as a market develops, consumers often become more discerning in their requirements, and if they are also becoming more prosperous they may be prepared to pay more for specialized products. The movement of particular markets is frequently directed by the economic standards which apply within the individual country concerned.

The U.S.A. is a prosperous country with living standards far higher than in the undeveloped countries of the Second and Third Worlds such as Nigeria. In the U.S.A. the toilet soap market may be in maturity or decline as consumers demand, and have the resources to pay for, specialized creams and lotions. But in Nigeria many consumers continue to use hard soaps and have not yet progressed to toilet soaps. Here the toilet soap market should have many years of growth ahead of it.

It follows that before attempting to apply this golden rule we need to be sure of our market, and this may mean we will be concerned with a market sector applying within a defined area.

The Time Period of the Market Stages

The time period of the various stages, and in particular the growth stage, is of major significance within the working of this golden rule. When considering the rule many observers are apt to think in relatively short time periods – three years of growth, followed by three years each for maturity and decline, is often thought of as a typical market pattern.

Some markets, and this applies particularly to market sectors, do have a relatively short life. The more rapid pace of technological and economic development over recent years has acted to shorten the life-span of many of the newer markets.

But it must also be appreciated that many markets have very long growth stages. The U.K. high suds washing powder market, for many years one of the biggest grocery markets in the country, was a growth market for some 40 years. The U.K. total toilet soap market was also in growth for a very lengthy period, probably in excess of 40 years.

The U.K. fabric washing market provides an example of how the time period of the growth stage of a market sector can change with the more rapid pace of technological development. As quoted above, the original high suds washing powder sector was in growth for as long as 40 years (from 1920 to 1960). The low suds powder sector which followed it was in growth for some 20 years. Then came detergent liquids which were a growth sector for 6 or 7 years. The concentrated powders have followed and it will be interesting to see for how long they remain the main growth sector.

The time period of the mature and decline stages of a market can be of great consequence from a financial view. If you accept the golden rule then these periods are the time when you recoup the major investments you have made during the growth stage. And if you are the leader, or a leading participant, you will have a strong vested interest in ensuring the stages continue for as long as possible.

Why is it Advantageous to Build Your Brand's Market Share During the Growth Stage of the Market?

■ *The answer to this question centres on the fact that during the growth stage of the market there will be a continuous flow of new customers entering the market. Their minds will be open on the market at this time, and their judgements will not be biased by a period of using and becoming attached to any particular brand. Later, in all probability, they will become biased in favour of the brand or brands they have used and with which they have become familiar. During the growth stage of the market it may be necessary to invest heavily, but the cost per new introduction is likely to be lower than at any other stage.*

The first brand sampled by the consumer acts to set a standard with him. If he is impressed and becomes a repeat buyer then to get him to change to another brand it will need to promise and deliver better value. And if he is to be converted to the new brand, it will need to offer more than just marginally better value.

The manufacturer who gets to the consumer first has the opportunity to make a strong and lasting impression. The first time a new product is used it is invariably a special occasion. There is an opportunity for the manufacturer who is first to make his brand name synonymous with the main benefit the product category brings.

Given that the brand represents an attractive proposition for the new customer, and its price/cost structure is sound, the new volume promised by the introduction should soon repay the cost of the sampling operation.

If the brand fails to provide a reasonable proposition and the new introductions fail to repeat purchase, then there will be no repayment of the introduction costs. But this is, of course, an argument against introducing the brand at all, and not a case against the timing of the introduction.

When the market reaches the mature stage the number of new consumer entrants will be limited. To build market share at this time it will be necessary to convert users of other brands. This is likely to prove difficult and costly. To tempt them to try the new brand, it may be essential to provide a substantial incentive. And the brands in possession of the market are likely to defend resolutely. In these circumstances most of the advantages are with the defendants.

If the competitive advantage the new brand possesses is of real significance it is possible that the entry during the mature stage will be a success both in terms of market share and ultimate profitability. But if the same brand had made entry during the growth stage its market share success would have been much more pronounced, its cost per new consumer lower, and it would ultimately have had a longer time period for 'taking profit'.

■ *There is less risk involved in investing heavily in a brand building operation during the growth stage of a market as against an invest-ment in the mature or decline stages.*

Judging with any confidence the time period of the mature and decline stages is always very difficult. If the market is overtaken by a new and markedly better technological development then maturity and decline can be of very short duration. To have invested heavily in buying market share during a mature stage that turns out to be of very short duration, and is followed by a rapid decline, could prove to be both a very costly and unsuccessful move.

Building Share in the Early Growth Stage of a Market – U.K. Fabric Softeners

The U.K. fabric softener market has become a most valuable fabric washing ancillary market, and also a major market in its own right within the total U.K. grocery business.

In the mid-1960s there were already thriving growth markets in fabric softeners in the U.S.A. and in parts of continental Europe. U.K. manufacturers were studying the developments very closely – the general view was that this category could also become a major growth market in the U.K.

In the 1966/67 period both P&G – *Downy* – and Lever –*Comfort* – launched fabric softener brands into the U.K. market. Both brands were given extensive support – sampling, heavy advertising, strong promotions, and in-store merchandising. However, the market development was most disappointing. Despite the extensive invest-ment from the two big operators the growth through the period 1966/69 was very poor.

In 1969 P&G withdrew its *Downy* brand from distribution. During its short period in the market it had probably incurred a considerable loss.

Lever considered the withdrawal of *Comfort* but decided against it. The company reasoned that the losses the brand had incurred were behind it. Beyond this there was a confidence in the company that the market would eventually 'take off' and that it was important to get leadership during the early growth period.

For a period of some 4 to 5 years Lever was the only major company with a brand in the U.K. fabric softener market. Colgate – *Softlan* – entered in 1973 and P&G – *Lenor* – came back into the market in 1974. This 4 to 5 year period was a vitally important one for Lever and the brand *Comfort*. The market moved forward appreciably. (In 1969 it was approximately 3,000 tons in volume and by 1974 it had grown to approximately 35,000 tons.)

As the only major brand, *Comfort* claimed the bulk of this market growth – and it was obtained relatively cheaply. Beyond this Lever was able to establish the *Comfort* brand as synonymous with the main benefit within the market – the *Comfort* promise, which was featured strongly and gained wide acceptance, was, 'Softness is a thing called Comfort'.

The total U.K. market for fabric softeners continued to grow through the 1970s and 80s. But now with three major manufacturers and the distributor brands competing it was more costly to obtain market share.

The Lever action in acquiring market share and volume through the early growth stage, and then growing with the market, served the company well. In the early 1980s, in a much larger total market, *Comfort* held a share of approximately 40% and outsold its nearest rival by nearly 2 to 1. Lever had followed the golden rule and it had proved to be right.

The Growth Stage of the Market – Price Influences

One of the most important influences on the development of a market is the level of the prices which apply within it. Price is one of the key factors within the 'best value' concept. Price movements, up or down, can have a material effect on the consumer's evaluation of the product or brand concerned.

Most consumer goods markets start with price at a relatively high level, and with demand restricted in part by this price. However, as demand develops and knowledge of the product/brand and the benefit it delivers becomes more widespread, a position is reached where the potential of the market becomes much clearer. The economies in unit cost that large-scale manufacture and distribution can provide become evident. To get these economies, sales volume needs to rise (i.e. the market needs to expand). To get this expansion advertising and promotion may be necessary, but in particular unit price needs to fall.

Judging correctly just when during its growth stage a market reaches this position is extremely difficult. An analysis of the current market, of consumer attitudes and views, of production and distribution costs, and extensive consumer price testing these and other studies can provide guidance. In the final analysis a sound feel of the market will be most helpful.

■ *The manufacturer who judges this market growth period correctly, and who has a brand which is well positioned, with sufficient production facilities and resources to finance the operation, can mount a move for market domination.*

If he is successful he can buy market share at what should be a reasonable price, and go on to lead the market through its maturity and decline.

The decision to make such a move is clearly a strategic one. Timing will be crucial and effectiveness in operation essential.

Should Market Share Ever be Built During Either the Mature or Decline Stages?

The answer to this question must be a very firm "Yes". Of course, there will be occasions when it makes very good business sense to build brand share during the mature stage. Indeed, in exceptional circumstances a business case could be made for building brand share during the decline stage, but it would be a very exceptional occasion. So much will depend on the particular market and on the competitive position within it.

It is important to appreciate that while this golden rule advises that you build your brand share during the growth stage of the market, it does not specifically advise against building during, for instance, the mature stage.

Of course, it will be necessary to consider whether the additional share will be worth the additional investment. This will require estimates of the movement of the market through maturity and decline, and also of the various expenditures that may be necessary. There could be a considerable risk involved, but, nevertheless, it could be a worthwhile exercise particularly if a lengthy period of market maturity and decline is foreseen.

Attempts to build brand share during the mature and decline stages of the market normally meet the problem of changing the buying habits of consumers who have become very firmly attached to their current brands. To move those consumers a brand competitive advantage is unlikely to be enough, a significant advantage will be necessary. Advantages of this kind can rarely be obtained without extensive investment.

■ *Attempts to make a major advance in a brand share during the mature stage of a market can be successful. But the risk and cost of such a move are likely to be very high. Any business proposal for such a move should receive a particularly rigorous examination. This golden rule, as are all the others, is 'right' on by far the majority of occasions – the best time to build your brand market share is during the growth stage of the market.*

Should Profit be Taken During the Growth Stage of the Market?

The golden rule fails to mention profit when it refers to the growth stage of the market, and so gives rise to this question.

In many markets it would be accepted that a major share development project, such as the launching of a new brand, would require support for up to three years (i.e. it is unlikely to make a contribution to profit in its first two years and may make only a small contribution in year three). It must be emphasized that this is a general statement. In some markets it is possible to make profit even in the first year, and in others four or five years may be necessary before profit is possible. But two to three years is the more generally accepted position.

The growth stage of some markets can extend over many years, sometimes as many as twenty; it would clearly have to be a most exceptional project for an operator to wait for twenty years before taking some level of profit return.

Once again we have a golden rule which is a very simple, uncomplicated statement that deliberately avoids detail. A more detailed statement of the golden rule would be likely to say something about profit taking in the growth period. Possibly a statement on the following lines would apply: "During the growth stage of the market you are advised to think in terms of investing a higher proportion of your gross margin in brand market share development and taking a lower level into profit contribution. During the mature and decline stages you should think in terms of taking a higher proportion of your gross margin into profit with a much lower level going to brand development and maintenance."

This statement is a more practical exposition of the golden rule. In taking profit the issue is more likely to be one of degree i.e. how much, between the various market stages rather than an absolute profit or no profit position.

■ *There is invariably a great difference between the ultimate profit delivery of a brand that is a dominant market leader as against the contribution of one that is merely a market leader.*

The opportunity to move a brand to a dominant position is a very special one – to miss it could prove to be a very expensive miss, for the opportunity is unlikely to be repeated.

This form of opportunity is most likely to be available during the early period of the growth stage of the market. The statement "Get the lead early and then be sure you at least grow with the market" sums up the position. If additional investment is required to move a brand through to a dominant leadership during this period (i.e. early growth stage) then it could well prove very worth while. A lower level of profit, possibly no profit, could be justified.

Of course, the decision as to the level of profit to be taken at any particular time is essentially a 'key' management judgement decision. For brands occupying the lower positions in a market the decision is normally an easier one. The general approach is to 'follow the leader' and from a commercial view this is usually a wise decision. There can be times when it is appropriate to worry the leader, and to make him 'sweat'. Such times need to be selected with skill and prepared for with considerable care.

For the leader the decision can be a more difficult one. He needs to ensure his brand continues to grow with the market – indeed, he may see a need for his share level to improve – but at the same time he may have a requirement for a substantial level of profit.

How should he handle this position? Much will depend on his circumstances and the competitive positions which apply within the market. The pace of development of the market will also be a factor of considerable significance. The size and value of the market, and in particular its potential, together with the strength (both financial and operating) of competitors and the importance of the market to them will also be of major consequence.

The use of a low brand unit contributory margin has already been discussed under the golden rule which considers stopping competitors entering a market. The same considerations apply to thwarting the efforts of competitors already established in the market. If the leader's margin is low then the contribution available to his competitors for brand development and promotion will also be low. However, if the leader is to maintain a satisfactory level of profit himself with low unit margins he will need a high volume, a volume considerably higher than that of his competitors.

To make the 'low unit margin' approach work the leader will need to have a dominant position. A position of marginal leadership is unlikely to bring a satisfactory level of total profit contribution. This is why many operators appear to prefer an approach based on high-level brand advertising, heavy research and development, and medium/high brand unit margins. They believe the advertising will work effectively to expand the market, and the product development investment will act to keep them ahead with consumers.

If you are a dominant brand market leader the low-margin approach has much to recommend it. It does not mean that you need to be under-invested in either advertising or research – your superior volume should provide a satisfactory level of total contribution out of which appropriate levels of advertising promotion, and development can be funded. But your competitors, with their lower volumes, are unlikely to be able to afford such investments.

The 'higher margin/higher advertising' approach can facilitate the entry of lower priced brands. In many developed countries it has helped to spawn the development of distributor brands (brands marketed by store owners through their own outlets). In a number of markets in the U.K. distributor brands have taken well over 30% of the total market – this is a very large volume to be *lost* by the 'branded' entrants.

If you have one of the smaller brands in the market then you are likely to be under pressure at all times if you are to make an adequate level of profit. Your best approach will probably be to search for a suitable 'niche' position and then attempt to ride with the market. You will almost certainly need to invest to develop your chosen 'niche' but if you do it effectively then your position through maturity and decline should be a reasonably profitable one.

The Importance of the Mature and Decline Stages

The growth stage of a market is invariably full of action and excitement. There are new brand launches, major re-launches, price activity, strong advertising and aggressive promotions. But with market maturity should come peace and profit.

This is the picture often painted of market development, and in many instances it will prove to be reasonably accurate. On occasions the 'battle' will continue into maturity – it is possible a new innovation of consequence will appear – but, in the main, peace and profit should be in evidence.

A frequent development is for a new sector to begin to grow within the total market. This new sector will attract the research and development effort, and also the marketing resources, of the market contestants. In toilet soaps in the U.K. the main market, covering complexion care and cleansing, has been in maturity and decline for a number of years. However, the market sector for special moisturizing creams and synthetic toilet bars has been in a growth stage. Advertising for the new products is to be seen frequently, as are special trial offers, and no doubt the research and development laboratories are working full out to get the next worthwhile advance in product performance.

For the 'ordinary' toilet soaps, advertising is less frequent (for some brands it is non-existent), trial offers are rarely ever used, and research and development effort is minimal. Beyond this, as the consumer interest falls and attention on the market declines, it is possible that price sensitivity will be less acute and so the brand unit gross margins can rise.

All of this means that the profit per unit during the mature stage should be much higher than during the growth stage. And the effort required of the operator concerned is very much less.

The mature stage of the market can clearly be a highly profitable one for the operator who wins the market share war during the growth stage, providing it lasts for a long enough period of time. Judging just how long the mature and decline stages of the market are likely to continue for is clearly a 'key' part of the considerations as to how much it is worth investing to establish a strong market position during the growth stage.

Very few major markets disappear overnight, but some do go rather rapidly. This is often so where fashion is deeply involved. There is a strong argument that in the future, with a higher level of research investment and with an accelerated rate of technological development, markets will tend to rise and fall more rapidly.

In the decline stage the profit level per unit for sales in the market should be at its highest level. There is unlikely to be any promotional investment, or any research and development. Brand maintenance cost should be very limited. As the decline progresses so the strength of the dominant leader should increase – ultimately he could be the only brand left in the market as the stores drop the slower moving brands from distribution.

There is a skill in protracting the market decline and doing so without making unduly high expenditures. Clearly, if the brand market leader has this skill he should benefit greatly. In fact, the dominant leader of a declining market should get an excellent return from his brand particularly during the earlier part of the decline.

Sometimes the Decline Stage of a Market Can Be Both Long and Profitable – U.K. Hard Soap Market

An outstanding example of the golden rule BUILD YOUR BRAND SHARE DURING THE GROWTH STAGE OF THE MARKET – TAKE YOUR PROFIT DURING THE MATURE AND DECLINE STAGES in operation is available from the U.K. hard soap market. It was a growth market for some 40 years, from before 1890 to about 1930. It was in maturity from, say, 1930 to 1945. From 1945 it went into a long decline. But there is still a U.K. hard soap market, albeit small, in the 1990s.

During the 1930s the Thomas Hedley company (owned by P&G) were very active in the market and invested strongly in their brand, *Fairy*. The brand became the market leader. *Fairy* continued as market leader into the war years and on through the 1950s, 60s, 70s and 80s. It still leads the market in the 1990s.

By 1995 the U.K. hard soap market will have been 50 years in decline, and the *Fairy* brand will have been the clear market leader for the whole of this period.

Throughout its decline stage, with the major contestants very actively concerned with soap and detergent powders, the hard soap market has been a relatively quiet one. Brand theme advertising has been limited, brand promotions few in number, and in-store activity negligible.

Many of the small/medium-sized grocery stores in the U.K. have for a number of years stocked only one brand of hard soap – the brand has invariably been *Fairy*.

For almost 50 years the *Fairy* hard soap brand has enjoyed a profitable decline. With a reasonable level of unit margin and a low level of promotional support, the absolute amount of profit earned by the brand over the years must have been very considerable – a reward for the hard work and investment of the 1930s.

This Golden Rule Applies to All Brands in the Market

The best time to make a move for brand market leadership is during the growth stage of the market. This would now seem to be generally accepted. However, it is important to appreciate that this golden rule applies to all brands in the market, and not just to the brand attempting to become market leader. This does not seem to be so widely accepted.

Irrespective of your market position – should you be No. 3, No. 4, or even at a lower level – the best time to make your major effort to improve your brand market share position is during the growth stage of the market. All the various favourable factors, such as the flow of new customers coming into the market, apply for all the competing brands. For all brands, the growth stage is likely to be the time when new users can be obtained at the lowest cost per new introduction.

Irrespective of the position of the brand in the market, progress made during the growth stage should mean a more profitable maturity and decline. And if you are conscious of competing brands making progress and you want to stop them, you had better do it during the growth stage of the market. It will be much more difficult, and more expensive, to push them back during maturity or decline.

Again a golden rule is tendering very good advice. Whatever your position in the market the best time to improve it is during the market's growth stage. You may need to invest heavily to get the desired results but the cost per new introduction is likely to be lower than at any other time in the market's life-span.

The mature and decline stages should be relatively peaceful, and unit profit margins should be increasing as the stages progress. But these are not periods for sleeping – skilful and shrewd management can extend them and ensure they produce the highest possible absolute level of profit.

Chapter 10

The Time to Stop
a Competitor is
Before He Gets Started

it's cheaper, in every way

If a potential competitor builds a new plant with the specific aim of entering your market, then the probability is that he will follow through and use the plant. And he will do this even though you may take a series of major defensive moves with your products/brands.

The market-place battle that is likely to follow will, in all probability, prove very costly. The result may be a major change in the market share positions with an extensive longer term cost to you. Even if the competitive attack is repelled there could be a very considerable short-term cost. Possibly, worst of all, the battle could degenerate into a longer term price war.

At the centre of your problem will be the fact that the new competitor, having invested in the necessary plant, may be prepared to sell at prices well below 'full' cost for a lengthy period. Indeed, he may reason that as long as his sales revenue is above his marginal cost he will be better off than he would be with an idle plant.

If the competitor had been stopped before he invested in his plant then the whole costly exercise could have been avoided.

This illustration, in a very simplified form, provides an insight to the business reasoning behind this golden rule.

■ *In by far the majority of instances it would be advantageous for an operator holding a strong position in a market to stop any worthwhile competitor before he 'gets started'. In fact, it would be worth his investing considerable time, effort, and resources to ensure that he does not 'get started'.*

'Before He Gets Started'

Before we move into the wider discussion which this golden rule attracts it is necessary to define what is meant by the phrase 'before he gets started'. Is it a reference to started on a research project, to the building of a plant, or to actual entry to the market?

The aim should be to stop the competitor before he makes any investment whatsoever. His researchers may have studied the market, considered the brands involved, made rough estimates of the various costs and revenues likely to be incurred, and other work that would normally be termed as 'desk research'. From this research the best result for the operator in possession is that the potential competitor should decide against any further action.

It may be argued that it does not really matter exactly when the competitor decides to withdraw as long as he does not enter the market. It is only when he enters the market that he begins to cause real trouble and to force expenditures to be made in defence. It is at this stage that brand volumes and market shares are threatened; it is at this stage that both short- and longer term costs are likely to be incurred by the defending brands.

If the competitor follows what might be termed as a logical economic approach he will review his position as he progresses toward the market-place, and he will continue these reviews when he has actually entered the market. The reviews will include a consideration of his financial position and other key indicators, and if at any stage they indicate that his best interests are to withdraw, then he will do so.

But, of course, competitors rarely ever follow a completely logical approach. They are often led by men and women who are very human in their approach, and who from time to time can be somewhat illogical in their actions. Often, after investing heavily in a project they are loath to withdraw, and the more they have invested the more reluctant would be a withdrawal. If they have carried out extensive research and development they want to use it, and if they have built a plant they will almost certainly want to go into production and enter the market.

■ *It may not be logical, but in very many instances the statement "The more they have invested, the more reluctant they will be to withdraw" is correct. Frequently such factors as pride and stubbornness are allowed to play a disproportionate part in the investment decisions.*

How to Stop Your Competitor 'Getting Started'

As we shall see later when we discuss the 'illogical competitor' there is no way in which you can guarantee to stop a competitor entering your market. However, there are a number of moves which you can make which should act to dissuade him from entering.

The best way to 'stop' a particular competitor will tend to be specific to him. It will depend on his position and his strengths and weaknesses. There will frequently be occasions when the operator who leads a market sees his main competition coming from a company that already operates in the market, or in a series of markets that are closely associated. In such a case the operator would be fully justified in taking a particular form of defensive action if he has reason to believe that it will 'stop' the competitor from making an entry.

In many cases the leader is concerned to stop not only the limited number of competitors who are already operating in, or close to, his market but also other potential competitors who are looking for 'attractive opportunities'. There is an obvious need to appreciate that the new competitors can come from outside the country where the market is situated (i.e. they may be international operators with a substantial interest in similar markets in other parts of the world).

It follows that in most markets the leader will need to cover his position against any specific competitor, and also in terms of wider and more general competitive approaches. Some of the more widely adopted means of attempting 'to stop competitors getting started' are:

1. Level of profit available;
2. Brand positioning;
3. Legal protection;
4. Effective research and development investment;
5. Advertising investment;
6. Build a reputation as an effective and efficient business operator
7. Bluffing.

1. Level of profit available

You make sure that whenever a competitor examines the market with a view to entry he reaches the conclusion that he will *not* make a satisfactory level of profit return on his investment.

The leader of a market, and this applies especially to a dominant leader, normally has the privilege of deciding the level of brand margins that will apply in the market. If he decides to take a high unit margin then, in effect, he is allowing others who compete in the market to take relatively high unit margins. (Note: This assumes that all the competitors have roughly the same level of effectiveness and efficiency in operation.)

Should the leader take a low unit margin then everyone else in the market can expect to have low unit margins and their profitability will also be at a lower level. Much will depend on the absolute volume levels which apply. The absolute margin level will be high if the volume is high – the leader should be well positioned, but his smaller competitors will struggle.

Where the leader takes a high unit margin he could be providing a form of 'umbrella' for his smaller competitors. In effect, he will be keeping them in business.

Clearly the leader's pricing policy is one of the key factors which determine the level of profit available in the market. If a competitor wants to take a large portion of the profit available he will need to offer the customers in the market better value than the leader. This means he must offer either a better quality product or a lower priced product.

To offer a lower price will be extremely difficult. His volume at the outset, and probably for a lengthy following period, will be much lower than the leader, and volume is likely to be a key factor in achieving a low unit cost.

A low unit margin policy will normally provide the leader with a strong protection against a price attack. A competitor considering entry to the market will quickly come to appreciate that if he is to make a satisfactory level of return on his investment he will need a competitive advantage which is strong enough to overcome a price differential – competitive advantages of this strength are not easy to come by.

It can be argued that following a low unit margin policy will mean that the leader restricts his profit to an unduly low level. This, of course, will depend on a number of factors including the volume of profit involved and how it relates to the investment that has been, and continues to be, involved.

What is a satisfactory level of profit in a particular circumstance is very much a judgement consideration. A higher unit price will not necessarily mean a higher total level of profit – the higher price could have a detrimental effect on brand volume.

The leader will need to take great care in deciding on the price level he is to use. Clearly he needs to make a satisfactory level of profit, but he will need to guard against taking too high a level. The advice "Don't be greedy" has much to commend it.

In considerations of this kind the competition within the market will obviously be of consequence. The strengths and weaknesses of competitive businesses, the ambitions of their owners and/or managers, and in particular their financial position, will be factors to be considered.

The stage of development reached by the market should also be a significant factor. One of the golden rules of strategy reads BUILD YOUR MARKET SHARE DURING THE GROWTH STAGE OF THE MARKET – AND TAKE YOUR PROFIT DURING MATURITY AND DECLINE. If you accept this rule then you are likely to adopt a low unit margin during the growth stage of the market, and then to widen the margin during maturity and decline.

■ *As we shall see, there are a number of other approaches open to the leader to stop his competitor getting started. However, to ensure that the competitor quickly comes to the view that an adequate level of profit will be extremely difficult to obtain must rate as one of the most convincing arguments.*

2. Brand positioning

It can be argued that all the subjects listed within this sector are part of business strategy: here we are concerned with a very specific strategy consideration. If you have the brand leader in a market then you clearly have a very strong interest in protecting its position. As the market leader the brand will be offering the consumer the benefit/s demanded by the main sector of the market.

One of the major acts of protection is to ensure that the brand leader continues to deliver this benefit at a satisfactory level and at a competitive price. Beyond this the leader will need to build protection from what is often referred to as a 'flanking attack'. Under this form of attack the competitor launches his brand into one of the smaller sectors of the market. He will hope to establish the brand in a strong position and eventually to move it nearer the main sector and challenge the leader.

One way of building protection against a 'flanking attack' is to move brands of your own into the various speciality sectors. It will then be very much more difficult for a competitor to enter such a sector and to build a strong brand, and it will be particularly difficult to build a brand that has the potential to attack the leader.

Any potential competitor who does not have available the resources to challenge in the main sector but who nevertheless studies the flanking positions and finds they are already occupied may well decide to stop before he gets started.

3. Legal protection.

The legal protection referred to is that which applies under the law generally but in particular under the patent and copyright acts. If the manufacturer can obtain a strong patent for the brand formula, or for the process that produces the product, or for any other important factor within the brand or product, then he will have provided himself with a degree of protection which could be decisive in 'stopping a competitor before he gets started'.

Very good examples of the law acting to stop a competitor are readily available from many industries; among those frequently quoted are examples in pharmaceuticals. The protection provided to a drug manufacturer for a particular brand is often very clearly shown and has, on occasions, been the subject of considerable debate. Some observers argue the patent law provides the drug producers with a protection which acts too strongly in favour of the producers against the best interests of the community; the drug producers, and they have allies, do not agree.

Specialists in the field of patents seem to be agreed that if a patent is to be effective in providing a defence and thereby stopping a competitor before he gets started, two considerations are important. First, the subject matter of the patent must be of consequence and, second, the patent must be constructed and registered skilfully.

If the subject matter is not of consequence there is a strong probability that any potential competitor will quickly find a way around it. Indeed, it can be argued that a weak patent encourages competition in that it invites an astute operator to challenge it.

There is a considerable skill required to draw up the actual patent statement in such a way that it provides the maximum possible level of protection and does not leave loop-holes that can be exploited by perceptive competitors.

Some operators are active in filing many patents, some of them relatively unimportant, in an attempt to cover a particular product area. They contest vigorously any known infringement of one of these patents, and they ensure that all potential competitors are fully aware that they will take legal action if withdrawal is not forthcoming. In this way they add a form of 'reputation for legal action' to their extensive patent protection – the two factors can act to strengthen the defensive cover.

4. Effective research and development investment

In a market where the products are based on a considerable input from research and development, the leader who is able to demonstrate that he is prepared to invest heavily under these headings, and has a performance record which shows he has been very effective (i.e. he shows that he is 'good at it' and gets results), will certainly be issuing a warning to competitors, or potential competitors, that he has no intention of allowing his products (and in turn his brands) to be surpassed by new technological developments.

It should be stressed that there needs to be evidence that the leader is effective in his research and development. Merely to be investing heavily is not enough. Indeed, if he is known to be ineffective then he will be wasting resources and thereby weakening his position. It is also necessary that the research and development effort should be directed into the 'right' areas. And the 'right' areas may change as the market develops.

Investment in research and development is more likely to deter new competitors. The establishment of an effective operation in this area can be expensive and require considerable time.

Existing long standing competitors are more likely to be aware of the extent, and effectiveness, of the research and development effort and also in which particular areas it is directed. If these competitors have been following a systematic 'competitor observation' approach they may well have picked up information which will enable them to estimate with reasonable accuracy where the research is directed and how far it has progressed.

5. Advertising investment

Under this heading the reference is to the often quoted 'barrier theory'. It normally features when consumer markets, where advertising is a major factor within the marketing approach, are considered.

The 'barrier theory' argues that in a market where the leading brands advertise heavily any new brand attempting to enter the market will have to invest at least at a similar level if it wishes to be successful. It follows that if your brand is a leader, and you are prepared to accept the 'barrier theory', then you will believe that by maintaining your brand advertising at a high level you are making it very difficult for any new entrant to challenge your position with any prospect of success.

If the new entrant wants to get his brand message home to a satisfactory number of consumers he will need to be sure that his voice is heard. He will need to shout at least as loudly as the leading brands in the market.

As a form of support for the theory, it must be accepted that by far the majority of successful consumer brands are supported by advertising, and that market leaders do tend to invest at relatively high levels.

It is also a fact that many of the smaller operations who make an unsuccessful attempt to introduce a new brand into an established market which is dominated by a limited number of big brands claim that their lack of success has centred on their inability to match the leaders in terms of advertising investment.

However, a closer examination of the smaller operators' problems will often show that their real difficulty is centred on the level of risk their projects carry. The risks are invariably very high and so it has proved difficult to give the brands the comprehensive level of backing they require to compete in the 'big league'. Their product competitive advantage has often proved to be very limited, and incapable being protected. They invariably have difficulty in raising the necessary capital to back their operation. This is often the real 'barrier' to their entry to the market, not the level of advertising.

■ *The 'barrier theory' of advertising is often mentioned, but it is difficult to find any hard evidence that it actually works in practice.*

Nevertheless, there can be little doubt that the level of advertising investment applying in a particular market will be a factor of significance to a smaller operator considering entry. If the level is high then the small operator may be 'frightened' – it could mean that he defers entry, or positions his brand so that it is not in direct competition with the highly advertised brands.

The big operator, accustomed to trading in markets where advertising investment is high, is unlikely to be frightened. However, the advertising level could act to persuade him against making a direct attack on the leaders. It may mean that he decides to make a 'flanking' attack, hoping to move to a direct attack on the leaders at a later date.

An additional reason, and for many operators a very strong reason for using advertising as a form of defence, centres on the view that advertising is probably the leading 'tool' for building brand personality. And brand personality is known to be a major consideration in helping to build brand loyalty.

Every brand has its own personality. One of the skills of a successful operator is to ensure that the personality he builds for his brand is one that is considered 'right' by his customers and potential customers.

Brand advertising should encourage trial, give assurance and confidence to existing brand users, and it should help to develop brand personality. It is this last consideration which has influenced many operators to prefer advertising investment as a defence rather than, for instance, lower brand unit margins.

6. Build a reputation as an effective and efficient business operator

If you build a justified reputation as a strong, effective, and efficient operator then you will command respect and potential competitors will certainly 'think twice' before they challenge you. It will also help if you are seen to deal 'ruthlessly' with anyone who does move against you.

Should a competitor mount a test market, how you deal with it will be noticed by other potential challengers. If you are soft in your actions they may be encouraged to consider entry. If you are strong and vigorous in your defence they will be aware that any effort on their part will require an extensive investment and may prove to be extremely expensive.

■ *Whatever kind of business encounter you are likely to meet you will always be better positioned if your business is managed in an effective and efficient manner. This applies particularly to straightforward battles for market position.*

The condition of your plant and other production facilities will often be seen by competitors and potential competitors as a signal as to how you view the future of a market or market sector. If you have allowed your facilities to become outdated and generally run down then it will be thought that you have decided the market has little future.

However, if you have maintained your facilities in a very good order, modernizing them as appropriate, and adding extra capacity, then your view of the market will be seen as one which looks for growth and development. You will have demonstrated your confidence in the future and you will have backed your view with your own money.

There is also the basic fact that plant that is modern and well maintained could make a major contribution to ensuring you are an effective and efficient operator.

Under this heading of achieving a high level of effectiveness and efficiency it is strongly recommended that every manufacturer, and in particular an established market leader interested in protecting his position, should carry out an exercise which calculates the 'optimum' unit cost of production for his brand.

Manufacturers are used to working with what are often termed as 'actual costs' (i.e. the costs that actually apply at a particular time). They also often use 'standard costs' (i.e. the costs that would apply given certain 'standard' conditions of performance).

The standard costs are normally used within management control systems. By comparing the actual cost against the standard, a guide is obtained as to how effectively management has performed in buying or operating the particular expense item concerned. The standard cost would usually be a level that good management would expect to achieve in the circumstances which apply.

'Optimum' costs are very different in that they are at the levels which can be expected to apply in ideal conditions and with optimum volume. Thus, for instance, standard costs may allow for volume at, say, 60% as this is known to be the level which is expected to apply. 'Optimum' costs would allow for volume to be at 100%. Breakdown allowances under standard costs may be at, say, 10% of machine running time as the plant is known to be old. 'Optimum' costs would allow breakdown allowances at say 2.5% as this is known to be the correct level for a new plant.

The construction of an 'optimum' unit cost for each brand has two particular values:

a. A comparison of 'optimum' with actual will show where savings are available if particular action is taken (e.g.

breakdown costs could be greatly reduced if plant is renewed
or unit cost could be greatly reduced if volume is raised).

b. The 'optimum' cost is the level a competitor could expect to
achieve should he work with, for instance, new plant, efficient
staff, and a high volume level.

Where the 'optimum' unit cost for a brand is well below the level of
actual unit cost, the manufacturer clearly has a major incentive to
improve his position. A high level of savings could be available to him
if he takes appropriate action, and his competitive position, should he
be attacked, will be much stronger.

7. Bluffing

At some time or other every business engages in at least a small
degree of bluffing. It may not be intentional, but it happens – even in
the most 'correct' of organizations.

When a businessman puts forward a strong, somewhat optimistic,
view of the position of his brands, and is less forthcoming on their
weaknesses, then he could be accused of bluffing. You could justify the
statements he has made if you share his optimism, and in any case the
statements would probably include phrases that make clear he is
expressing a personal opinion which has limitations. Nevertheless,
he will have emphasized certain points strongly and in this way acted
to build up a particular position.

Sometimes the bluff will be more deliberate. Operator A may talk
loudly and frequently of his proposed entry to a specialist sector of a
particular market. In fact, his action in this sector is a relatively small
and insignificant one. His big effort is in another sector which he has
been most careful not to mention. His aim has been to bluff his competitors to get them to commit resources to the defence of their position
in the sector he has talked of, and to leave him with a much easier and
surprise entry to the sector he has not discussed. His aim has been to
use the 'bluff' to gain a competitive advantage.

There can be little doubt that skilful bluffing can on occasions help
the attacker. Variations on the simple example set out in the previous
paragraph will be known to operators in a whole series of markets.

Can a skilful bluff also help to stop a competitor getting started? The answer must be very clearly "Yes".

When a competitor is considering entry to a market he is likely to make a series of calculations covering the financial and market strength of those in possession of the market. The 'actual' figures are unlikely to be available to him and he will need to make estimates. The estimates will be based on the various pieces of information available, and a degree of 'bluff' may be contained in this information.

Similarly, bluffing can be part of the information disclosed on the extent of the research and development investment made by the existing market leader, and on the product developments he expects to have available as a result of the investment.

Of particular importance, a mixture of 'limited disclosure' and bluffing can act to hide the level of profit the leaders are taking from a brand. Normally companies are not required to disclose the exact level of profit contributed by a particular brand, and so skilful bluffing can be used to either increase or decrease the level of the estimates.

Bluffing can help to deter a potential competitor but it needs to be used with care. In attempting to evaluate competitive statements, or announcements in the press, it is always important to differentiate between opinions, forecasts, and hard facts. There is an enormous difference between "If we consider the conditions right it is possible we may make an advertising investment as high as £1m for this project" and "We have made an advertising investment of £1m for this project".

If it is to work the bluff must be believable. If an advertising investment of £1m is realistic, a statement which hints at £3m is unlikely to impress. If the same bluff is repeated a number of times then competitors will quickly come to read it and take appropriate action.

■ *It would normally be most unwise to rely entirely on bluffing if you wish to ensure that your competitor does not 'get started' in your market.*

Bluffing is most likely to be a marginal factor which could help you to gain additional protection, but your real defence is more likely to be successful if it is based on one or more of the approaches set out above.

Of these various defensive measures that an operator may employ the one that is likely to be most effective is the one that makes it very clear to any potential competitor that he will have great difficulty in making a worthwhile level of profit from his efforts; in particular, that he will have difficulty in making what he is likely to consider as a reasonable level of gross profit (i.e the difference between his sales income and his direct cost of production). This will mean that he will have very limited funds to pay for advertising and sales force, product development, and other promotional approaches – and possibly nothing at all left for a net profit.

In effect, this means that the man in possession of the market is likely to be taking a low unit margin, and that he relies on his volume to ensure that he has a satisfactory level of profit.

■ *In practice business operators who wish to stop competitors from 'getting started' in their markets appear to use a combination of the approaches listed.*

They may make high-level investments in research and development, ensure their plants are kept in a state of high-level productivity, and also maintain a strong level of brand advertising investment.

In some industries (e.g. pharmaceuticals) legal protection is of great significance, together with strong research and development.

In all industries it is most helpful to be an effective and efficient operator. And, occasionally, a little skill in bluffing may be useful.

The 'Illogical' Competitor

There is a very strong rumour that a certain company intends to enter your market, and that he is intent on challenging your leadership position. You have already taken action to stop the potential competitor from getting started, but the rumours continue to persist.

All the indications are that the company's interest in your market is 'illogical'. The available unit margins are considered to be low, the market is certainly highly competitive, and there do not appear to be any openings for a new brand in the market. But the rumours persist.

If this potential competitor should make his move it will mean a very costly period will follow for everyone in the market and in particular for the leadership brands. And this cost will be incurred even if the new entrant proves unsuccessful. What further action could be taken to avoid the costs?

Firstly, all possible legitimate actions should be taken to check the rumours. Do they have any real base? Where do they come from? Just how much verification is possible? These questions, and many others, need to be asked and answered. The aim should be to get a firm confirmation or a dismissal of the rumours.

It is important that there should be a comprehensive review of the company concerned. In particular the review should cover the resources available to the company, and a consideration of its management and operating performance.

If the company is a sound one with a successful management then even though the move appears to be an 'illogical' one it must be treated with full respect. The strengths of the company should be reviewed in detail. Is there anywhere it could use its strong positions to make a successful market entry?

In particular the brand development plans should be reviewed. Is there a worthwhile product improvement that can be brought forward and launched into the market at an earlier date? Are there any outstanding cost savings available if special action is taken? Are there new avenues of distribution that could be developed?

In effect, every effort should be made to ensure that no 'easy' road of entry is available to the 'illogical' competitor.

In the final analysis, if a competitor, 'illogical' or otherwise, decides he is going to launch into a particular market irrespective of the costs involved, there is no way the leaders in the market can stop him. And this is surely exactly as it should be. However, there is no reason why the market leaders should just sit back and have their position eroded. It is in their interest that the attacker should pay dearly for any market share he may gain. This way he may come to rue his move, take care not to repeat it, and have great difficulty defending any gain he has made.

When You are Not Concerned to Stop a Competitor Before He Gets Started

The thought that a market leader would be pleased to know that a competitor is planning to enter his market and that he should not be concerned to stop him is one that is very difficult to accept.

Where a market is undeveloped it is possible that a company which does not have the resources to pay for the development is prepared to accept a competitor entering and helping with the development task. Of course it would ideally like to select the new entrant with considerable care – the aim would probably be someone who would be a so-termed 'good competitor'.

There could be an argument for accepting a competitor who was not necessarily 'good', but who was at least prepared to invest and expand the market. Out of the growth the man in possession should be able to claim a substantial share without paying heavily; in fact, it could be additional volume obtained at a low price. But into the medium/longer term the new entrant could pose a threat; life would never be really peaceful again.

It has been argued that where a big company dominates a market it can be very happy for small operators to enter with new developments. The theory is that if the new entrants show signs of being successful the big man will be able to copy them rapidly and then out-market them with his superior organization and more extensive resources. In effect, the big man is allowing the new entrants to do his test marketing.

Of course, there is always the risk that one of the smaller new entrants may enjoy enough success to survive and go on to become a real competitor. There is also the argument that a large dominant leader would be pleased to have a degree of competition for public relations reasons. A monopoly, or a near-monopoly position, in any market is likely to attract official investigation and almost continuous review. Again the man in possession would certainly like to select his competitors – a move that is most unlikely to be acceptable to the authorities.

It must be recognized that there are circumstances, normally very special circumstances, where a leader is prepared for a competitor to enter his market and that he will not take any extensive action to stop him. However, such instances are rare and, in general, the man in possession is much more concerned to stop any potential competitor before he gets started.

The golden rule THE TIME TO STOP A COMPETITOR IS BEFORE HE GETS STARTED is clearly excellent advice. There are many ways you can do this but probably the most effective is to ensure that he finds it very difficult to see any prospect of making profit from those markets where you are trading profitably and intend this to continue into the future.

Index